LOPE DE VEGA
AND SPANISH DRAMA

WORLD DRAMATISTS
In the same series:

WORLD DRAMATISTS

LOPE DE VEGA AND SPANISH DRAMA

HEINZ GERSTINGER

Translated by Samuel R. Rosenbaum

WITH HALFTONE ILLUSTRATIONS

FREDERICK UNGAR PUBLISHING CO.
NEW YORK

*Translated, and adapted, from the German.
Published by arrangement with Friedrich Verlag,
Velber, Germany*

*Copyright © 1974 by Frederick Ungar Publishing Co., Inc.
Printed in the United States of America
Library of Congress Catalog Card Number: 72-90812
Designed by Edith Fowler
ISBN: 0-8044-2227-3 (cloth)*

862.3
Ξ 3̅ ∂̅

CONTENTS

For the convenience of the reader, all play titles are provided in English. Please see bibliography for Spanish titles and translation data.

THE COMEDIA:
ITS THEATER AND ITS TIMES

1. The Historical Background of the Golden Age

Exploration into the spirit of the times of any era is apt to lead one into directions that may be misleading. For instance, it would be wide of the mark to regard the flowering of Spanish drama in the late sixteenth and seventeenth centuries as the emergence of an artistic substitute for the lost political potency of Spain or as a form of self-delusion to conceal the decline in the vigor of its society.

In fact, the majority of the Spanish public, whose enthusiastic passion for the theater made this flowering possible, was just as impoverished before it occurred. The idea that theater was a form of bread and circuses to be maintained in order to quiet unrest among the people, as had been the practice of caesars and dictators in earlier times, was not the objective of the royalty and nobility. True, they were the main support of the theater, but this was because they themselves loved theater.

The same paradox applies to the church, which was astonishingly tolerant of even the most frivolous plays. It did not feel it was necessary to utilize the theater to promulgate its doctrines among a people who were in any event firmly Catholic in their beliefs.

The theater, or at any rate the professional theater, was rather a newly discovered form of the miming that had been traditional ever since Roman times, a form of public diversion like religious processions or bullfighting, for which a new repertory had to be devised. It was therefore understandable that many writers placed themselves at the service of the stage. Not least among their reasons was the fact that it was profitable.

The typical example of this was Cervantes. He began to write plays only because he needed the money, not, as he himself said, for pleasure, but gradually he got to enjoy it. A century later this theater was no longer in existence, but the works of the great dramatists among them are still alive to this day. The political and historical reasons advanced for this golden age of the theater are therefore at least questionable.

Perhaps we had best focus on the theory that the conviction of devout Spanish Catholics that all life is merely an illusion is evident throughout the comedia.

Indeed, at first glance it might seem rather farfetched to interpret the plots of the numerous cloak-and-sword comedias as symbolical. Their writers might have meant to indicate below-surface dimensions only in extremely rare cases. But the impression cannot be lightly brushed aside that we see here a manifestation of a certain unconscious attitude toward life. To be sure, the Spanish comedia was a medium of entertainment in the simplest sense—it was performed to please and to satisfy the desire to see a play. In this it was quite contrary to the demands of the modern theatergoer.

2. *The Social Life of the Day*

The important historical events between 1469, the date of the unification of Spain by the marriage between Ferdinand of Aragon and Isabella of Castile, and the ending of the Hapsburg rule in 1700, had far less significance for the Spanish theater than has previously been assumed to be the case. Only secondary influences, such as the conversion of feudal knights into a caste of courtiers, and the strong interest of Philip IV (1621–1665) in theater, had a direct impact on the life of the theater. But the structure of the society was hardly altered by such external catastrophes as the loss of the Netherlands (1581) and the defeat of the Armada (1588).

This structure was fundamentally different from that in other European nations. It was the product of its special historical background and development. By the seventeenth century the western European nations had consolidated their boundaries. Spain, however, had for some centuries been engaged in a conflict with the Moors, who were in possession of the southern half of the Iberian peninsula and who, by reason of the length of their occupancy, felt equally as entitled to southern Spain as the Christian population did to northern Spain. Because of the Moorish domination Spain did not follow the cultural development that occurred in the rest of Europe following the victory of Charles Martel over those very Moors in 792. Instead it accepted and adopted much of the highly advanced Moorish culture. This was not without significance for Spain's rapid economic rise in the sixteenth century.

The military functions of the knights of France and

Germany filled only a portion of their lives. They had long been accustomed to acting as the bearers of their national culture, while those of them who were without intellectual resources carried on as robber barons on their own. By contrast, the Spanish knight was everlastingly engaged in active conflict. He continued not only to carry on his military activity, but also to act in the true sense of his old knightly obligation to protect and defend the poor. Peasants and city dwellers could not have survived without this protection. It was necessary for them to accommodate themselves to submission to authority, a posture that they came to take for granted. This brought about in the people an attitude inimical to any kind of revolution. This mentality was paralleled at a later time by the respect of the nobles for royal authority.

The need for continual national defense, the uncertainty of the future, and the consequent insecurity of all worldly belongings, impressed themselves on the knights as well as on the lower classes. Life was an adventure. Only the abstract values were real. All reality was only an illusion. Faith and honor were the only irreplaceable possessions.

It was clear that certain kinds of progress could not develop under these circumstances. The merchant, as well as the laborer, who had to maintain his existence, sometimes even by shady expedients, was disdained rather than accorded respect. This led to these occupations being infiltrated by foreigners. Trade and commerce were looked down upon as necessary evils. Any form of work was considered ignominious. This principle, established by the nobles, retained its efficacy even in later, changed, times. All earthly needs were despised. Even family life was not essential.

It is apparent that the church stood only to gain in external and internal power over a people who were fundamentally unbelievers. The organized authority exercised by the church forbade the slightest trace of disobedience or heresy. It corresponded to the military authority exercised by the knighthood. For the impoverished masses, at any rate, the true faith was their great comfort, one that offered them the attractive assurance that the next world was the only way out from the insecurity of this one.

At this point let us address ourselves to concepts that were of great importance in the influence they exercised on Spaniards.

Purity of race, the authenticity of good ancestry, was the first requirement for becoming a member of the nobility or for holding office in church or state. Proof of such descent had always to be evidenced. Racial purity could be asserted only by individuals who had no trace of either Moorish or Jewish blood in their veins. This first outcropping of fanatical race prejudice in Europe could be traced back to two underlying motives: the fear of the intellectual superiority of the Moors and the Jews, and the contempt for all foreigners as unbelievers.

True, the acceptance of baptism protected Moors and Jews from persecution by the church organization. But it did not protect them from social ostracism because it was recognized that most of them submitted to baptism not from religious conviction but for reasons of expediency. The instrumentality that conducted decisive warfare against everything un-Christian (which was regarded as equivalent to un-Spanish) was the Inquisition. Basically, the Inquisition was an early form of secret political police, a system of spies and informers that none could evade. Its original mission was defense against all foreign influences, above all those that were Moorish or Jewish, that could undermine political or religious belief. It was only after the Reformation had established itself successfully in northern Europe that the Inquisition took up the warfare against heresy. Here the motivation was the fear that Spanish heretics might act as agents for enemy powers rather than the fear that the Reformation would put down roots.

The consequence was rigorous supervision of all intellectuals, scholars, and artists. A severe censorship of books was initiated. In order to counter this, many writers, and especially employees of printers, enrolled as officials of the Inquisition as a means of protecting themselves personally from persecution. The Inquisition became a huge secret apparatus. To retain its power and authority, it found it expedient to cater to the appetite of the masses for entertainment. The notorious autos-da-fé, in which the unhappy victims were exposed in humiliating costumes and obliged to confess guilt in public, were among the great entertaining spectacles Spaniards could never see enough of.

Biased historians in later centuries pictured Hapsburg Spain as the bulwark of darkness and superstition where the most horrible cruelties were perpetrated. They regarded Spain as the last relic of the Middle Ages in a Europe that had achieved a totally different outlook under the influence of Protestantism and of humanism. Such a historical view overlooked the fact that the Inquisition and its doctrine of racial purity were only one facet. At the very same period in this ostensibly reactionary kingdom a cultural peak was being attained such as Europe had rarely known. The era of grand inquisitor Torquemada and Philip II was at the same time the era of Velázquez, El Greco, Cervantes, Lope de Vega, and Calderón. The era of Pizarro was at the same time the era of Saint Theresa of Avila.

Contradictions are, to be sure, characteristic of every Mediterranean people. When, however, they become so extreme as they did in Spain, political, religious, or social sundering will occur if a release in a superior power that is acknowledged by all and is accepted by all as decisive is not found. In Spain the containing factor was the generally accepted belief in the frailty of all earthly possessions, in surrender to a higher power that is at the same time one's only safety and security. For if all cares and intrigues in this world are only an appearance, then our inmost soul is invulnerable and is protected in the last resort. All earthly life is but an illusion. Man can only win through to reality if he stands the test in the midst of danger, in time of privation, or in moments of powerful emotion. What man achieves or what he accomplishes is of no consequence. How he conducts himself is what most matters. Life is an adventure into which we must plunge in order to find ourselves. The unmasking of men, the disillusion of life, these are the moments of self-realization.

Even the commission of sin does not necessarily result in one's being rejected as an outcast. It is only a kind of testing. The path of survival from such a test is penitence. A current generated by opposite poles pulsates through the life of every individual. The robber becomes a saint; the voluptuary becomes an ascetic. This does not happen because it is believed that character either in real life or on the stage should develop this way. It happens because of the forces outside one, influences that the true believer recognizes as the bestowal of grace but the skeptic names the working of chance.

We must keep this basic concept before us in order to comprehend the situations we meet in the Spanish comedias. It is the writers of these comedias who hold the mirror up to the adventures they depict in their plays. Thus they show us the servant who serves to counterbalance the impractically idealistic hero. These servants act like their masters, but from entirely opposite motives. The servants are always mindful of their creature needs. The chivalrous ideal of the nobility is contrasted with the practical realism of the masses.

At first glance we might come to the superficial conclusion that the dramatist's intent is to show the contrast between the wealthy elite and the poverty-stricken multitudes in a setting that will lead the observer to draw a critical sociological observation. But on closer examination we realize full well that the aristocrat's wealth was far from being impressive. Actually the noble cavalier was often poorer than his own underlings.

In very truth, the nobleman was often painfully poor if he had not succeeded in landing a lucrative office for himself or a member of his family. This would be considered his own fault because it was the result of his obedience to the tradition that he was not supposed to engage in any form of gainful employment. It is significant that, in spite of the limited material prospects, elevation to the nobility continued to be so sought-after a goal.

There were three grades in the upper classes: grandees (of superior rank); titulos, or holders of titles (of lesser rank); and hidalgos (or gentry). The hidalgo was a sort of rural knight or landholder whom the comedias loved to deride. The hidalgo who held no office at the royal court, but because of Spain's conservative social immobility was not an authentic knight in the true old sense either, had no choice but to become a cavalier: one who devoted his life to matters of love and honor. But it would be a mistake to draw superficial parallels with the life styles of today and to equate such cavaliers with playboys as is frequently done in modern productions of the Spanish comedia.

Quarrels for love or honor were conducted subject to a code of rules observed by the upper classes that was not the less strict because unwritten. It was in the time of Alfonso the Wise (1416–1458) that the law was passed permitting a husband who surprises his wife and a lover *in flagrante delicto* to kill them both on the spot. A father had the same right over his daughter, a brother over his sister, an engaged man over his betrothed. The courts attempted in vain to combat these barbaric but nevertheless strictly observed conventions. To be sure, their own judgments were not of the most merciful. According to them, the husband had the right to confine to his house as slaves the guilty wife and her lover. Instances are recorded in which the cuckolded husband, instead of punishing his erring wife and her lover, would use the situation to extort all possible advantage for himself out of it.

The scholar Joseph Gregor rightly described it as an extraordinarily complex and severe code of gallantry. He wrote:

> If a cavalier with a lady were to burst suddenly into a home and declare to the proprietor that he was compelled to protect her, the owner is supposed to surrender the rooms at once to these

guests and remove himself. If the lady is in a disguise that conceals her identity, and the cavalier is not known to the home owner, it is entirely possible that a wife would be aided in committing adultery in this manner in her husband's own home.

Such situations of course lent themselves admirably to the composition of comedias. To what extent such situations are indebted to the assimilation by the Spanish of Moorish customs is an area that remains to be thoroughly explored. It is well known, from authentic accounts of Spanish life as well as from the comedias, that part of the code that treated principles of honor contained provisions that were frequently counter to Christian commandments and compelled the individual to compromise with his conscience. As the self-confidence of a Spaniard was also dependent on the good opinion of his community, he was compelled to set the laws of his honor above his religious convictions. Killing to preserve honor was a duty in the world he lived in, even if it was a sin before God. A cursed duty, indeed, but an obligation.

Tirso de Molina distinguished between "honor," that is, moral or ethical honor, and "honora," that is, honor as defined by society. In practice, however, hardly any distinction was made. The honor of a loved one was defended as zealously as the honor prescribed by religion. Duels were commonplace occurrences. The effort to forbid them by law could not alter this state of affairs.

After all, the lives and morals of the Spanish nobility, as well as of those of the lower classes who aped them, were ruled by form without content. What made sense in the past—a past in which knighthood flourished, in which one lived unquestioningly by the principles of the strict code of honor, the defense of faith against unbelief, the pursuit of heroic adventure in which one protected right against wrong by one's own unaided right arm—had become in late sixteenth-century Spain, when the country had become more stable, an illusion of an ideal, a sort of sporting affectation for its own sake.

Anyone who still took creed of the past seriously became a figure of tragedy, a Don Quixote. The adventuring cavalier was, to be sure, an idler who out of snobbishness imitated the person of a nobleman like Don Quixote but who lacked his tragic stance. He followed the forms of this gallant code of morals, but not life itself, seriously. He had long since realized that all was only illusion, all only passing theater. In spite of their knowledge of the transitoriness of everything of this earth, what impelled them into their mad adventures was not despair but joy, not the fear of the desperate man faced with the meaninglessness of life but the sure knowledge of an ultimate haven of safety. The motive force of his conduct was not character or conscience but temperament and instinct. Character was governed by a religious belief that was beyond doubt.

The cavalier could abandon himself to the adventures of this world with the same ardor and passion with which he threw away all his possessions in order to lead a hermit's life in the service of God. The fight for the honor of his position and for the love of a fair lady found expression in battles for the honor and the love of God. Spiritual love called forth the same response from them as did the worldly. It was Tirso de Molina who perhaps penetrated most deeply of all Spanish dramatists into the hearts of men. It was he who provided as the leading motive of his works this "interplay of sensual and mystic love."

It was thanks to the joy taken in this game of illusion that the cultural life of this people bloomed in a period when its highest ideals were asceticism and denial of the real world. Such blooming would not have been possible if these ideals had resulted only in casting the people into despair. The fact that the delight in this game of illusion had its roots in the very belief that at the same time taught the ideals of asceticism and denial of the world is a paradox that is inexplicable to a skeptic of today. The cruelty of the Inquisition, the madness of race bigotry, and the arrogance of social position, diverted our glance for some centuries from that other Spain of the Renaissance and the early baroque. Now our awareness of its theater, its comedias and its *autos sacramentales*, shows us the other side of the picture.

The special quality of this Spanish culture was not its enormous sense of national consciousness. The culture of Spain's golden age (the *siglo de oro*) was, above all, a phenomenon of life in the cities.

Political and intellectual life in this period was concentrated in the big cities. The cities were the center of attraction for the younger generation of the upper classes, who set the fashion and who aspired to having gallant adventures as well as attaining preferment to office at court or in the church. In actual fact, the city of Madrid, which was elevated to the status of capital of Spain in preference to the older Toledo by Charles V in 1560, had in only a few decades become one of the leading cities in the world. In the seventeenth century it already had four-hundred thousand inhabitants. It was a city of international intercourse that can be compared only with, say, today's Paris.

The displays of gallantry that Lope de Vega and the other writers of comedias exposed in their plays were actually taking place every night in the narrow streets, under the latticed windows, and in the darkness of the city parks, so that the endless stream of comedias that was produced was for good reasons compared to a *chronique scandaleuse*. Madrid, the home of the royal court and of the highest church dignitaries, the very center of the Inquisition, was at the same time the most immoral and frolicsome city in Europe. This was true not only during days of festival and carnival when every kind of audacious mischief flaunted itself openly in the streets but all through the year. Even the number of loose women in the town is said to have wildly exceeded that in all the other big European cities. Lawbreakers had their own associations. They could be hired for any kind of lawless enterprise.

Toledo, the former capital, grew quieter and quieter while Madrid was growing apace and flourishing. Toledo did, however, continue for a long time to be a second national center, even in a cultural respect, maintaining its place at the core of serious religious art. The only serious rival to Madrid was Seville, a city bursting with the joy of life. It was of eminent significance for the development of the theater. And then, Valencia, which through the long sojourn of Lope de Vega within its walls, was to become the third great theater city of Spain. Out of the variety of cultures existing in it side by side, as was to be expected in a great seaport, it developed a special style of its own. "Here," wrote Karl Vossler about this metropolis, "the Arab Middle Ages and the Italian Renaissance encountered each other, and, between the two, stood the Provençal forms of life and of the arts." The old university towns, especially Salamanca and Alcalá, continued to have important significance for Spain's intellectual life. Scholars were increasingly regarded as members of a respected class of their own that also had a firm economic base.

Culture in Spain was not, however, as it was in other countries, the concern solely of the academic community and the gentry. It obtained at every level of society, not only through passive participation of the lower classes, but by their active cooperation in its creation. Painting and writing poetry became a passion that seized all classes—royalty, clergy, cavaliers, and manual workers. Even if it were only a fad, it was a fad in which the whole nation could rightfully take pride. The average Spaniard looked upon the arts, especially the art of playwriting, not as a specially creative activity, but as "an accomplishment that could be learned, copied, and indulged in." While this attitude showed itself to disadvantage in the disproportion between quantity and quality, it did create an aura that encouraged many to create works of art.

Pleasurable participation in cultural activities was universal regardless of the social stratum to which one belonged. The mere fact that the whole population was included in the cultural life proved the little man's independence of the dominance of the nobility.

Certainly the extreme poverty of the masses was as marked after the golden age as before. In the zeal of the cultural participation of the people, a parallel to the delusive escapism in which the upper classes indulged can be seen. The illusion of participation in the arts deluded the masses into disregarding reality. In this illusion the little man had his own satisfying adventures. He fled from the narrowness of his own life into the world of the theater. The contrast between the life style of the onlookers and the style of life played on the stage can again and again be witnessed in the theater. One example is the predilection of respectable citizens for plays of risque character.

Lope de Vega, in his comedia *The Shoemaker and the King*, portrays a shoemaker and a king in friendly neighborly contact. When reading this we should bear in mind that Lope de Vega was writing about and for a society in which a noble could strike an importunate beggar dead without fear of punishment, in which a princess could kill one of her servants with her own hands. Year after year peasants were increasingly being deprived of their rights. Trade for the most part was carried on by foreigners. The mass of the people made a scanty living by doing odd jobs.

The economic decline was no longer to be stayed. A last blow to the economy was dealt by the edict of Philip III in 1609 compelling Moriscos (Moors converted to Christianity after the reconquest), who had been the most industrious workers, to depart from Spain. Anyone who could do so grabbed at any municipal or church job he could land. The number of church functionaries multiplied. If we look at this social misery side by side with the blooming of the cultural life, we can only conclude that the arts, especially that of the theater, were a substitute of fantasy for the reality being disregarded.

What actually did a Spaniard, whether he was a gentleman or a common man, have, from the broad social point of view, except a flight into illusion? They were all impoverished together. Even the kings were heavily in debt. But before the consequences of the Inquisition's bloody guilt led to the total downward plunge of the country, Spain once more experienced greatness through this indulgence in fantasy. This paradox of history can be comprehended only in the light of the Spanish character. As Ralf Styer wrote:

> Certain of a divine order that cannot be lost, they indulge in playing with unaffected good cheer and a southern serenity, although they are coupled with the same deep melancholy that still today is characteristic of Mediterranean man and his culture. He displays a spontaneous joy of life that is tempered by the inextinguishable consciousness of the ever-present proximity of death.
>
> If we keep this well in mind, we will appreciate the power of these poetical creations we study and find in them much more than merely a many-colored and harmless sport.

3. The Theater of the Comedia

Spanish comedia is an offspring of the stage, not of the writing desk. It has this quality in common with the other peaks in the history of the theater, the drama of ancient Greece and the stage of Shakespeare and his contemporaries. Experience proves that it is only the plays of these three epochs in the history of European theater that are generally accepted and performed as the really authentic stage plays of all time. The primacy of theater over the other fields of literature is the decisive factor. It is true that only the works of really gifted writers have survived the test of time, while those of the flock of routine dramatists have long been forgotten.

Delight in playacting is a characteristic of all the Mediterranean peoples. The innate love of miming was, however, often suppressed by alien influences and by changing religious concepts so that stage exhibitions sometimes came to be regarded as immoral and socially unacceptable in Italy and in Greece. In Spain theater continued to hold sway against all the tendencies to downgrade it. The reverence for miming inherited from pagan days continued to flourish without interruption in Spain even after Christianity had taken root. Spain is the only country in which dance as a part of religious observance and ritual was not only never prohibited, but on the contrary openly permitted.

We may seek to account for this phenomenon as an expression of an inherent characteristic of the Spanish people, but we must not lightly dismiss the assertion that it was due equally to a conscious hostility to Islam's firm opposition to any form of playacting. Though it was not feasible for Spaniards to indulge in theater in the fullest sense during the period of unrest and political insecurity, even in the early Middle Ages Spain was reputed to be "the classic land of troubadours and entertainers." The singers of that oldest and best-known Spanish form of poetry, the romance, were much more like performing actors than were the French troubadours or the German minnesingers.

The Spanish troubadours were not mere narrators. Their performances were enriched by gestures. Everything they presented appeared "heightened, sharpened, and compressed from mere narrative prose into short, decisive occurrences, impressive moments, and unexpected surprises" (Karl Vossler). The dramatic element permeated the act of narration from the outset. It required only some change in the surrounding circumstances for the recitation of the romance to become a type of theatrical presentation. It was a natural development for the recitation to become the work of a personal union between playwright and actor. Thus it was that the European theater was saved from becoming bookish, a threat caused by the misinterpretation of the rules of the drama of antiquity. The Aristotelian rules were ridiculed in Spain.

The second type of personal union, one that was typically Spanish, was that between playwright and priest. This averted the menace of clerical objections to theater that might have arisen here and there. Later, through the establishment of theaters belonging to various orders this union proved itself extraordinarily fruitful. The possible enmity of the church to the theater was conclusively avoided when the Feast of Corpus Christi was introduced in 1264. The procession to celebrate this festival gave Spaniards a religious vehicle by means of which they could express their "joy in the revival of the stream of life." In these processions, humor and dance, far from being forbidden, were expressly commanded.

In the popular idiom the feast was named the *fiesta de los carros* (the festival of the carts). As was being done in the early days of English theater, tableaux were drawn through the streets on carts. At first these tableaux were just figures of saints. Soon these were replaced by people in costume. Then it required only a short step to convert these tableaux into dramatic scenes. This scene, which began to be presented at the end of the Feast of Corpus Christi, became an *auto sacramental*. These *autos sacramentales* were discontinued in 1765, but such dramatic productions could still be seen in Valencia in the nineteenth century.

We must avoid regarding these *autos sacramentales* as serious, austere eucharistic dramas. They were saturated with comic scenes. Earlier efforts by the church to suppress the comic or farcical element from the realm of religious observance failed completely when the pope himself instituted the Corpus Christi festivals.

In 1535 Italian acting companies appeared in Spain for the first time. It is unwise to exaggerate their influence. Such productions at the royal court as the *Gli Suppositi* of Ariosto in 1548, performed at the marriage of Maximilian to a daughter of Charles V, were the exception. Even then the people preferred their own local players. In spite of all economic obstacles, a native theater sprang up with unprecedented vigor, one such as no other country in Europe had experienced.

Their stage and their settings were so primitive that it is difficult for us to picture them. At first each company was a one-man operation. Only after several decades were any of them able to get beyond this very limited level. As late as 1604 Agustín de Rojas wrote a melancholy report—one we should take *cum grano salis*—about the various acting companies:

> Bululu is a one-man traveling showman, who persuades the local priest to let him recite his comedia. The local barber and the sexton join in as listeners. He stands up on a chest and recites his piece, describing the entrances and exits of his characters as he goes along. The priest collects a few coppers for him in his hat. The actor gets a mouthful of soup and a lump of bread, and goes on his way.
>
> Naque consists of two players who wear beards of fur and are able to recite a couple of *loas*, or at most an *auto*. They sleep in their clothes, rarely get enough to eat, and never feel the bite of cold

or winter because of the vermin that infest them. In Aragon the price of admission is a copper.

Gangarilla has grown to a little troupe of three or four men. One plays the fool, another is the young man to whom the woman's role is assigned. They carry false beards and wigs. They borrow any female garments they need—at some risk to their owners. A seat costs a cuarto, but bread or eggs or other foods are also acceptable for admission. They always travel with their arms folded as they do not possess a cloak between them.

Cambaleo consists of a woman who sings and five men who howl. The woman is carried on a sedan chair. They hire a bed for her for any overnight stop. The others sleep on straw. The woman rations out any food they get. All five of them have only one napkin between them.

Garnacha is a company of five or six men, one woman who plays the leading lady, and a boy who takes the second woman's role. They carry their costumes in a chest loaded onto a mule, on which the woman rides backward. They sleep four in a bed, stay in one place for eight days. They give a private showing for payment of one chicken or four reales.

Boxiganga: two women, one boy, six or seven men. Repertory includes six comedias and three or four *autos*. They carry one chest for props, another for costumes. They travel with four pack animals, three to carry the two chests and the women, while the fourth is used alternately by the rest of the troupe. They like to sleep near fireplaces, to get close to the sausages hung up to be smoked.

Farandula travels with three women, eighteen comedias, and two chests of equipment. They eat well, only give performances in the larger settlements. They include a number of gallants and seducers, who swing their cloaks with an air, cast leering glances at the females, and beckon to them with gestures.

Compañia: this is a big company of well-bred and cultivated men with some quite respectable women in it. They must not lack capable players because all classes of people attend their shows. They carry fifty comedias, three hundred costumes, about twenty-five pounds of baggage, and travel only on pack mules, horses, wagons, or sedan chairs. They are not content with mere carts. There are sixteen actors, thirty persons in all who must be fed, and Lord knows how many more who are thieves.

This is not so very different from the description we have by Cervantes about the troupe of Lope de Rueda (died 1565), who was honored as "the father of the art of the Spanish theater." Nevertheless, he was able to carry his entire stage equipment in one bag.

Cervantes also left us a description of the theater of his day:

It consisted of four benches arranged around a square space. Six boards were laid over the benches so that the stage was raised four spans high above the ground. The stage setting was an old curtain that could be drawn to one side by two cords and provided a sort of dressing room. The musicians stood behind the curtain and sang any old ballad without guitar accompaniment.

The earliest permanent stages appeared, as they first did in England, in the *corrales* (or yards) formed by the adjacent courtyards of two or three abutting houses. Unlike the sequence in Elizabethan England,

however, these were not superseded by specially constructed theaters. The players continued to be guests
on private premises. Some improvement in their social
standing was thus brought about by their business
connection with a charitable fraternal organization.
Sodalities placed courtyards at the disposal of a theater
on condition that a separate admission charge be
collected. In this way the audience had to pass through
two controls, one that of the owner of the courtyard,
the other that of the theater management. This was
the first occasion in the history of European theater
when theater served the needs of community charity,
something that proved to be beneficial to it. In a later
development, the sodalities rented their courtyards to
a theater, so that the double admission charge became
unnecessary. The alliance with such monastic orders
was especially beneficial because it gave theater a shield
for averting hostilities or even prohibitions from
church sources.

The actual stage structure in these *corrales* remained
substantially unaltered. A front stage apron was cur-
tained off from a dressing room, or *vestuario*, at the
side. This varying stage setting itself was an essential
element. This complied with the wishes of the playwrights, who had a higher appreciation for imagination than for reality. In one of his comedias Cervantes
has a character describe the imaginary scene of the
play as follows:

> You are beholding a scene in which you can see
> London and Rome and Vallodolid and Ghent
> within a hand's breadth of each other. What does
> it matter to the audience if, without altering the
> stage in the slightest, I fly from Germany to
> Guinea in a twinkling. Thoughts have wings.

With them you can easily accompany me everywhere I choose to take you, and you will never be too weary to follow.

When Cervantes, in his *Don Quixote*, describes this very stage fantasy as deception, it does not contradict this quotation, because it is the parson who adopts this skeptical attitude. Since the parson is characterized as a sober, unimaginative, and realistic citizen, it is consistent with his character for him to pronounce a harsh verdict on the "untruths" of the theater.

To carry his audiences along with him, Lope de Vega himself asked for no more than four pads of paper, two boards, two actors, and one fine emotion. And when the structure of the primitive stage had, step by step, become sophisticated, he complained: "Our theater has converted itself into a picture frame for costumes and for nails to hang things up on."

Our contemporary style of staging plays once more aspires to establish the superiority of imagination over the technique of creating a realistic illusion. This has its counterpart in something that might appear to be unusual in the Spanish comedia, which was that, to counterbalance the extreme simplicity of the scenic background, the costumes were quite luxurious. In historical plays the Spanish actors wore gorgeous costumes. Though these costumes were those in fashion at the time of performance, the period in which the drama was set was evoked by a few characteristic details.

For a long time then the staging in the *corrales* remained extremely simple. Only by making use of the balconies on the back and sidewalls of the *corral* (*lo alto del teatro*) were the tower and the much-admired window scenes carried out. Occasionally, also, side curtains were hung up, which made possible additional entrances and exits when they were pulled apart. If they were drawn fully to one side one could see into the shallow space behind them. They were also used as a special trick to indicate a long journey by an actor. The actor would walk across the stage while the back curtain was pulled open so that behind it could be seen a prepared scenery, perhaps a monument, or a tomb-stone, or a rock, that would represent the place or environment required by the action. In this way also whole groups of persons could rapidly be made visible and made to vanish with equal speed.

The dropping of a curtain between acts was un-known. Instead, short interludes were staged, because the audience got restless if nothing were happening on the stage for even a short interval of time.

Allegedly, the first agreement between a sodality maintaining a hospital and a company of actors was arrived at in 1510 in Malaga. The theater there is said to have been founded by the archdeacon Juan del Encina. We know him also as one of the earliest notable writers of comedias. The first agreement for which documentation between a theater company and a sodality exists is one drawn up in Madrid in 1556. The first permanent theater in Spain, constructed in a *corral* in Seville, dates from about the same year. Lope de Rueda appeared there as an actor.

In 1579 the first continuously operating theater was established in the Corral de la Cruz in Madrid. A second followed in 1582 in the Corral del Principe. These stages were still the most primitive imaginable. Plays were given only in the afternoon. A canvas cover was spread to protect the audience from the sun. When it rained the show was canceled.

In 1587 Diego de Tapia, the Augustinian friar, demanded that stage acting be banned for religious reasons. He preached that all make-believe and therefore all art was only deception, inspired by Satan. Two years later the Jesuit Pedro de Rivadeneira raised his voice against actresses. "They sing like sirens and transform men into beasts." To justify his stand he quoted the hostility to theater of the early Christian Fathers, and described the stage as the devil's own pulpit. Both these attacks were unsuccessful. Most of the clergy was directly interested in the perpetuation of the theater. The emergence of great plays, the harbingers of the waves of great plays to come, won the support of even the most erudite.

The situation of the theater was more perilous in 1597 when Philip II ordered all theaters to shut down for two years to observe mourning for the death of his sister. This was seized on by opponents of theater as an occasion to make this suspension permanent. In 1598, after the death of Philip II, his successor Philip III summoned a council of state to discuss the question of allowing the theater to reopen. The consequence was that in 1600 the performance of comedias, but subject to certain restrictions, was allowed to resume. This concession was justified on theological grounds by quoting a statement favorable to theater by Thomas Aquinas and by referring to the financial benefits the sodalities could obtain through theater operation.

The first restriction lifted was the ban on stage appearances of actresses, as the archbishop of Madrid was personally of the opinion that the playing of women's roles by boys in female clothing encouraged immoral ideas. The last attacks on the theater from clerical sources were reported to have occurred in 1609. Even groups otherwise so hostile to each other, like the circle of Lope de Vega and the classicists, joined forces against them.

The last threat to the theater from the church ended with the accession of Philip V to the throne in 1621. All the arts, above all the theater, meant more to him than all his duties of statecraft. He wrote some plays himself. At his court, theater flourished. It achieved an impressive triumph of art over the political decline of the reign. Though theater came under the influence of the royal court, theater never became so exclusive a possession of the aristocracy as did the theater of the French or that of the petty princelings in Germany. It remained throughout conscious of its tie with the entire public.

This is evidenced by the installation of a theater on the model of one of the *corral* theaters in the royal palace in 1607. The local public was permitted to attend this, although the royal family saw the performances from seats in a concealed private box. The primitive stage settings used in the *corrales* were not regarded as adequate for audiences from the royal court or the church. Now the influence of Italian theater made itself felt. It led to the technically excellent productions in the late seventeenth century.

In 1638 the leases with the sodalities in Madrid were not renewed. From then on it was the city of Madrid that took over the leasing. That year can more or less be designated as the year of birth of the town theater. In 1624 the actors had formed their own Confraternity of Our Lady of Novena, which was the first European actors league since the organization of technical operators in the theater of ancient Greece. Meanwhile, the social position of the players of comedias, and the respect accorded to them, had been enormously improved. The smaller troupes away from the big cities continued to suffer misery and hunger in spite of the well-established renown and material success that the big respectable troupes had achieved. A Lope de Rueda could still be his own writer, producer, and director, although by the seventeenth century these functions were being divided.

We can perhaps recognize the rapid rise of the theater in public esteem in the first third of the seventeenth century from the rise of the notable actor Gaspar de Porres, who later became a director. As an actor he had entered into an agreement under which he was obliged to appear in every kind of play, in return for his residence, keep, and clothing *in natura*. In addition he received travel expenses and medical care if he fell ill, plus the sum of ninety ducats at the end of each four-year term of his contract. Later, as a producer he contracted to pay an actress a daily guaranty of six reals, plus sixteen reals for every play she acted in.

By 1619, an actor was earning fourteen and thirty-six reals a day, six hundred reals for Corpus Christi week, and the use of four riding animals. The renowned Maria Calderóna, the beloved of Philip IV and mother of his son, the younger Don Juan of Austria, drew a star's salary of one thousand fifty reals for four stage appearances and travel allowance for her spouse and her lady's maid. Payments for her costumes were even steeper; they often cost three hundred ducats, or seven times as much as Lope de Vega got for a whole play.

From these business facts alone we can conclude how the standing of the actor was valued above that of the playwright, of the stage above that of the play text. The common people, in spite of their own poverty, regarded these salaries and expenses as reasonable, not as unduly generous. They adored their actors and actresses with the same devotion bestowed on them in ancient Rome or offered today to their favored stars by film fans. Scraps of their costumes were eagerly taken home as souvenirs, and legends about the best-loved artists were spread in the current tradition of the times as though they were church saints. Francisca Baltasaras was the favored among the Spanish actresses who played boys' roles. When she died it was said that all the church bells began to toll of their own volition.

The arena where this public, so enamored of the stage, gathered to see their favorites in performance was a courtyard. The balconies and the windows of the houses surrounding it provided the galleries and the box seats. Men in the audience stood, not sat, in the pit or parquet. Women sat in a closed-off upper section, a so-called *carzuela* (coop), or *corredor de las mujeres* (women's gallery). By an ordinance adopted in 1608 certain performances in the forenoon were set aside exclusively for women. Behind the pit area for the standees, whose critical opinions were most influential, there were raised benches under a roof. In addition there were benches along the back and side walls of the building.

The admission price rose with the respectability of the enterprise. In 1600 it was about one real for the charity and one for the theater itself. By 1616 admission cost about double that. The prices for a box went up to thirty reals. The resourcefulness of the promoters served to build up the eagerness of the public for the shows. A system of subscribers was already known.

Plays were regularly presented only in the afternoons. They had to end an hour before sunset. The standees in the pit, the *mosqueteros*, decided on the success or failure of a play. The derivation of the word *mosquetero* is still uncertain. They were equipped with rattles, bells and whistles, and even cucumbers, which they pitched onto the stage to express their dislike. They were feared by all the dramatists. They were probably organized, so the intimation that one artisan in the audience exercised a sort of precensorship over a play may well be true. He was the one who gave the *mosqueteros* the signal to exercise their approval or disapproval.

The letters of the Countess d'Aulnoy contain details about the theater that strengthens my view that theater was regarded by Spaniards as a sensation, a kind of folk festival, not so bloody as a bullfight and not so tragic as an auto-da-fé. She reported bombardments of the stage with vegetables. She also wrote about the common restlessness among the spectators, especially among the women who sat in the *carzuela*, loose women who all through the performances tried to attract the attention of the men to themselves by tittering and calling out to them.

An official was stationed at every entrance to try to suppress any disorder. As at all public affairs in southern countries, sales of refreshments were actively continued during the performances.

Even if the account by Don Juan de Zabaleta is much exaggerated, conditions in the popular theater had not improved much by 1650, at a time when the best plays were being presented as formal court productions. His account describes the quarrels among the women in the audience, the bribing of ticket takers, and the competition for good seats. Zabaleta closed his report with these words:

> Everything degenerates into lamentations and looking for lost things. Those who sit near the doors can't hear and see the actors well; the ones in the last row can see the actors but can't hear them. The result is that nobody enjoys the comedia in full. During any play a great deal is spoken, so when you can't hear the words clearly, the action just can't be understoood. This means that for many, the comedia comes to an end as if it had never begun.

Even the most famous actors and dramatists were apprehensive of the verdict of the public. The public was always demanding new and newer plays. They wanted a new opening at least once a week. They did not want to see an old play, even in a new setting. The dramatists were forced to write a spate of new plays at a speed that has no precedent in the history of literature.

Rarely did a comedia end without an appeal to the audience for its indulgence. Lope de Vega himself was obliged to conform to this indispensable usage. Very rarely would a dramatist dare to antagonize his audience as did Ruiz de Alarcón, in the foreword to the first edition of his collected comedias:

> I address myself to thee, thou wild beast. Here thou hast my comedias! If they displease thee, it would please me to know it, for it would be a sign to me that they have merit. But if thou shouldst find them to be good, that would tell me that they are worth nothing. The money they have cost thee would give me joy.

We must not misjudge that public as being merely a rabble. This public certainly was more enthusiastic than the so-called educated public of subsequent centuries. The very fact that the same playgoer who occasionally witnessed one of the formal productions in the court theater, who was familiar with the technical advances and the elaborate settings of the baroque theater, who reveled in the *autos sacramentales* given at the Feast of Corpus Christi in the public squares, did not find fault with the niggardly equipment in his own theater of the people, that he actually wanted it to be preserved, testifies to an innately creative gift for appreciating the richness of fantasy. It was only travelers from abroad who decried the primitive quality of the native stages because they lacked the simple naiveté, which Goethe points out is the prime criterion of a discerning theater audience.

Karl Vossler described the Spanish theater audience very aptly:

> This thousand-headed, crowded, inquisitive multitude, eager and tense, was Lope's most important audience. We might be tempted to call them a half-educated or semi-ignorant big-city rabble, if we applied our present-day standard to them. But it would not fit. In the Spain of their day there were not yet our kind of urban mobs without the power of judgment, which have heard and read all kinds of stuff but not got to the bottom of anything, that do not know or believe or understand anything thoroughly, that are so lacking in consciousness of unity that they are like separately atomized particles. The horizon of those playgoers was probably narrower but sharper, more uniform and concentrated, so that their opinions and tastes were much more certain. They were

brought up by their parents and grandparents to be loyal Christians and Spaniards, all of the same church and belief. They had unshakable concepts and views, firm in their beliefs about honor, decency, morals, character, God, eternity, nation, nobility, matrimony, love, gallantry, fighting, bravery, folk wisdom, the exploits of Spanish heroes and great men, Spain's world domination, and Spanish America. All these things they felt in their bones. Lope's audiences were no proletarians. They exhibited the reactions and made the responses of a true and authentic folk. When the subject rose to the level of the spiritual, they became an integrated community, ardent and devout.

It was for this broad public that the best dramatists wrote, not for a limited elite of the intelligentsia. It was for this audience that the leading actors trod the boards in new roles every week.

The flowering period of the mutual understanding between erudite, brilliant, high-minded playwrights, and the standees in the pit of the theater, bloomed in the intimacy and genial give-and-take of the Spanish theater.

Theater was craftsmanship, but only the most well turned-out and attractive product could survive the critical requirements of the audience. In the *corrales* the whole nation lived out its illusions, not as a narcotic, not as an intoxicant, not to drowse itself into unconsciousness of its political downfall, but to please and satisfy itself and to reaffirm its belief that all life is only a game. This is why this theater became "the perfect expression of this society."

4. The Dramaturgy of the Comedia

Karl Vossler asserted that: "Though the formula that Lope de Vega and Calderón devised is firm and characteristic, the effect they had beyond the Spanish drama was exerted almost only through their motifs and their way of thinking, not through their technical methods." This is true to some extent. The charm exercised on us by the Spanish comedia in present-day productions can only be explained by our acceptance of the outlook on life that animated the Spanish dramatists. This outlook corresponds to the feeling for life of people not yet influenced by the Renaissance, people who had not yet adopted the Greek motto that "man is the measure of all things." In this connection it is only of secondary importance that as a devout Catholic the Spaniard recognized and acknowledged that the measure of all things lay in his conception of God. It was essential to him to regard man as an object, not as a subject. What was important was not what man wished, but what he was challenged to do. The determining factor was the situation in which he found himself, not the action or reaction that was of his own contriving. Insofar as this philosophy is expressed in the comedias, we can agree also with those who are so bold as to assert that the comedia of the Spaniards is timeless world theater.

Spanish drama was not invented in the sixteenth or the seventeenth century. It goes back to much earlier sources from which it developed. It would therefore be a mistake to make the *zeitgeist* the only explanation of its concepts and its techniques. We know that Spanish drama arose from a combination of mimetic and literary elements.

One point of departure was not the mystery play, almost uniform throughout all of Europe because of the predominance of the Catholic Church, but the mime of the wandering narrative singer. The other point of departure was the gradual transformation of chronicle into romance, of spoken poem into mimed narrative, and finally, in a more stabilized age, the conversion of narrative romance into dramatic presentation. *La Celestina*, that brilliant giant of a dramatic romance, illustrates graphically the point at which literature and theater meet. We find all the subsequent forms prefigured and germinally forecast in this composition.

The Italian influence, while limited, was yet strong enough to inspire a special class of Spanish touring actors, who, though organized like the Italian troupes, presented essentially their own topical jests and situations. The difference is clearly apparent in the plays and presentations by Lope de Rueda, in which he separates the *paso* (or interlude) from the balance of the play in order to develop in it possibilities of mimetic action quite uncontrolled by any literary restraint. In the *paso* he could better create figures of comedy that soon took on clownish traits than he could in the plays they accompany. The tragicomic note, unknown to the Italians, was a later development out of these ingenious improvisations and assumed decisive influence.

In fact, the Spanish interlude derives from still another source. As early as in the Middle Ages there were entertainments of that type during banquets and tournaments. There were also burlesque episodes inserted in certain church ceremonies. We can trace back to the thirteenth century the use of such short comic episodes to fill in intervals in festive performances.

From the simple *paso* emerged the *loa*. This was a type of self-sufficient interlude that was performed between the acts of the principal production. Sometimes it was replaced by the rendering of folk songs or folk dances, or the recitation of anecdotes. Later dramatists, especially Lope de Vega, incorporated these elements directly into their plays and utilized them as part of their dramatic material.

The Italian interlude tended to outgrow and suppress the play itself and to become in itself a dominating art form. The Spanish interlude, instead was absorbed into the larger comedia. Lope de Vega made use of these interpolations in especially exciting moments in the plot in order to intentionally heighten the suspense of the audience by an interruption of the plot. The use of such musical and dance forms is familiar to us today in the musical comedy, which makes use of all dramatic and mimetic possibilities, in order to achieve total theater. It would seem that the pure mime, acting, dance, and song are more effective than the mere spoken word alone to hold the attention of the audience. But this was not so with the Spaniards. For them the word was essentially more meaningful to the ear than to the mind. To them the sensual enjoyment of the sound of the language was even more important than its sense.

It was clear that humanism had to reject such exuberant growth of a folk theater. A theater was growing here in diametric opposition to the theater of antiquity as seen by the humanists. The triumph of the folk theater was assured not only by the limited interest the Spanish spirit took in the humanist trend but far more by the fact that the early Spanish dramatists championed these interludes although they were deprecated or at least slighted by the learned critics.

Cervantes has the personification of the Spanish comedia remark in his own defense: "I am really not so bad, if I don't conform to rules in the much admired works of Seneca, Terence, and Plautus, left behind for strict observance." And in his comedia *Pretense Becomes Truth*, Lope de Vega professed his feeling of obligation to please popular taste. Diocletian rejects the rules of classical drama in the following conversation with the actor Ginés:

> Ginés: Would you like me to recite Terence's *Andria* for you?
> Diocletian: Old stuff!
> Ginés: Then maybe Plautus's *Miles Gloriosus*?
> Diocletian: No, no, give me something more up to date, a good story.
> I favor the Spanish taste in these things.
> They are more ingenious, even if not so artistic.
> As long as they are more true to life,
> I don't bother about rules and precedents.
> In fact, strict rules of art only bother me.
> Sometimes I think that too faithful obedience
> To the rules completely misses truth to nature.

This confession to preferring "the Spanish taste" is also a humble, even if slightly ironic, tribute of the living theater to drama as a literary art. Only the literary form is considered art. The theater is mere artisanship. So is playwriting. None of the great dramatists was aware that by his self-confessed modest acquiescence in folk taste (which was also more profitable) he was in fact making a greater contribution to art.

Just as everything was guided by the potentialities of practical stage production, not by theoretical maxims, so also was the division into types of plays. From an aesthetic point of view, we would have to categorize them differently, or rather we should establish a principle of uniformity in the various types, regardless of whether the tragic or the comic element predominates. But the essential characteristic of Spanish drama is the intermingling of both elements, even in the religious drama. So let us look at the division into acts that was prevalent in the time we are discussing. This means, in essence, the time of Lope de Vega. At that time the writers classified their plays into three different types of comedias. Later, after Calderón became active, into six.

The classification into three types was for the convenience of the producers, so they could decide which actors to employ, which costumes and settings would be appropriate, for the play in hand. For this reason a distinction was made between the spectacular *autos sacramentales* staged at Corpus Christi celebrations and the simpler *autos sacramentales*, the *comedias de capa y espada* (cloak-and-sword plays), and the *comedias de teatro* or *comedias de cuerpo* (situation plays).

Cloak-and-sword plays could be mounted without the need for any transformation machine. No special setting was required; a few screens or background curtains sufficed. As the plays were always set in the present, they needed no more costuming than garments of the day.

The staging of a *comedia de cuerpo* was far more difficult. A type that lay midway between the secular and the religious categories, it required special apparatus to present the numerous miracles and allegories. It was expected that the costumes would at least suggest the dress of the period in which the play was set and they had to be especially splendid, for the audience was more interested in the theatrical effects than in the plot of the story.

Later, dramatists thought in terms of six categories: (1) the cloak-and-sword play; (2) the situation plays (*comedia de teatro* or *comedia de ruido* or *comedia de cuerpo*); (3) the *comedia de santos* (with saints as characters); (4) *burlescas* (broad farces); (5) *fiestas* (like outdoor fêtes); (6) *comedias de figurón* (of character).

Cloak-and-sword plays dealt with situations in private lives. Above all, characters in them were not supposed to be of higher rank than the gentry or lesser peerage. In the *comedia de teatro*, however, princes and kings could appear, so many of these take their subject matter from history. The *comedias de santos* staged legends of the saints. The *burlescas* were broad farces or frivolous trifles, sometimes parodies on elevated subjects. The *fiestas* were bigger festival productions, something like the open-air celebrations in the royal palaces. The *comedias de figurón*, the newest category, were modeled on the lines of the French comedy of character. This classification left out of consideration the clearly religious plays and the *autos sacramentales* because those were never played in the theaters.

The term comedia is the generic term for the Spanish baroque play. When discussing Spanish drama the labeling of plays as comedies and tragedies in our modern sense is not practical because of the common interpenetration of the comic and the tragic elements in each play.

It seems to me that this book will be most useful to the contemporary reader if I focus on the cloak-and-sword comedia. For with the exception of Calderón's dramas few serious plays, such as perhaps Tirso de

Molina's *The Trickster of Seville* (the Don Juan saga), or Lope de Vega's *The Village in Flames* are still being performed. And the short farces, with a few exceptions, such perhaps as the interludes of Cervantes, are of more interest to theater historians than for their practical impact on contemporary theater.

The derivation of the name is simple enough. The *capa*, or cloak, the outdoor garment of the cavalier of any chivalric pretentions, was not only the garment that witnessed to the superior social standing of its wearer, even if he were only aspiring to social standing, but also an impressive theatrical costume. A circular cape is beloved of actors even today; it can be swung most effectively to express a passion in gestures. The *espada*, the sword, was similarly a possession of every cavalier in that duel-disposed period. It was an indispensable and necessary stage property for the theatrical combats so often occurring on the stage.

Cloak-and-sword plays were, in fact, the least costly of all to produce, and they were the most artistically satisfying for the dramatists to work up. Even dramatists so antipodal in their thinking as Lope de Vega and Suárez de Figueroa were agreed on that point. This was because such plays made their effect on audiences not by elaborate sets or stage properties, but solely through the imagination of the writers. For this reason they were also called *comedias de ingenio*. On the other hand, the writing of one of the *comedias de cuerpo* or *comedias de santos*, with their miracles and sensational effects, could be done by any neophyte bumbler. But these opinions were all changed after Calderón's plays came out.

It was the ambition of Lope de Vega to uplift and purify the cloak-and-sword plays into a form of dramatic art, to make them appeal to an educated audience. The manner of plotting seemed adequate to him. As they were already filled to overflowing with unexpected turns and surprises, he would concentrate on the dramatic structure of the presentations.

Before Lope, each play was introduced with a prologue and a statement of the plot. It was then broken by interludes, or *loas*. While these half-improvised interludes had some thin relation to the dramatic development of the plot, Lope believed the time had come to work them, in some way, into the principal plot. The actors should no longer offer the audiences interludes they had prepared themselves but should play them as roles that would fit appropriately into the principal plot. The text became, if not dominant, at least an element of equal importance, in the *Gesamtkunstwerk* (Wagner's word). Concentration on the structure made whatever remained of the improvisations previously prevalent fade out.

Even in Lope's earlier plays the characters on the stage often had little relation to each other. They simply took turns in addressing the audience. The derivation of this form of theater from the earlier traveling shows of buffoons and jugglers was obvious. It was only through Lope's own artistic development that he was able to transform these informal productions into a basically integrated dramatic form. Instead of the actors performing "to the public," he had them performing as a unit "before the public." This became possible only when the dramatist succeeded in focusing the attention of the audience on the plot instead of allowing it to remain, as it was before, on the actors. Thus Lope effected a reform in the taste of the audience itself.

Lope's cloak-and-sword plays have innocuous subjects for their plots. Many start off from some familiar adage, some well-known folk tune, some local usage or custom. His plain audiences, just as audiences do today, preferred to see life as they knew it and fashionable doings and gallant conduct on the stage. It was Lope's genius for dramaturgy that converted scenes from society life into sparkling theater. Vossler wrote: "Chance and coincidence play a major part in the structure of Lope's plots. The popular approval of such elements accounts for the widespread popularity and survival of his plays." The significant point, however, is that it was precisely Lope's imagination that enabled him to create effective stage plays out of chance and coincidence.

To make these comedias work as theater, he did not write the usual prologues and interludes. He reduced the number of acts from five to three or four. He only retained the essential closing appeal to the audience, the request for its indulgence for the play. But he wanted to retain the theatrical effect that up to then was obtained by the interludes. Working the folk tunes, the dances, and especially the topical verses and allusions directly into the action itself, he endowed these elements with a dramatic function. These passages served to heighten the suspense of the audience by slowing down the development of the plot.

Each play of Lope's averages between three thousand and thirty-two hundred lines. It takes two and a half hours for each to be played. In the manual *The New Art of Writing Plays* (published in 1609), he offered the principles of his method of playwriting. He repudiated the practice of following the form of ancient Greek drama, urged a mixture of the comic and the tragic elements, and opposed so-called art by the natural. He did not feel the need for handling time plausibly. As for the three unities of classical drama, he found valid only the dictate about plot.

Tirso de Molina made the same recommendations in his *Defense of Spanish Comedy*. He defended the Spanish formula, pointing to the agreeable mixture of the comic and the tragic elements, against French attacks. As for the classical unities (time, place, plot), he asserted they are obviously unviable. The illustration he used as proof is the impossibility of handling a love story dramatically in this framework. He pointed out: "How can any two intelligent people fall madly in love with each other, give each other proofs of their tender feeling, and then celebrate their marriage before sunset, all within twenty-four hours?" His argument is one single defense of the superior rights of imagination. The plot must proceed toward the final solution. The audience knows it has to end well, but it does not know how the satisfactory solution will be arrived at. It is this feeling of expectancy that heightens the suspense and keeps alive the interest of the audience.

This is the same sense in which Lope's prescription is to be understood. Lope wrote: "The solution must be held back until the final scene, because if the audience knows what the final outcome will be, they will begin to look for the door to the exit and not bother to wait three hours to find out." About the structure of the play he wrote: "The situation must be posed in the first act. In the second one must interweave the strands in such a manner that by the middle of the third act nobody can guess what the outcome will be even though the direction was hinted at."

The basic form of the plot can almost be described as a geometrical figure: two or more pairs of lovers, and their attendants, are the characters on the chessboard. In a chess game the parallel or intersecting plays are guided by an overall plan of campaign. In a comedia the obstacles to be overcome and the ultimate objective to be achieved are handled in a like manner. The characters conduct themselves as if reflected in a mirror, frequently as if seen in several mirrors cracked or broken. Cavalier A and his servant and Cavalier B and his servant act basically in the same way, though on a different level.

This special Spanish dramatic form, which might be called the "mirror play," is unique in the history of European drama. It is closely bound up with the whole outlook of Spaniards on life in general. In the comedia, the focus is not on the final objective. It is on the behavior of the individual characters in attaining it. All the characters are bound up with each other; they constitute a geometrical polygon, each angle of which is connected with every other.

Accident and chance play an essential part. But these accidents are not just awkward dramatic contrivances. They are the miracles of the everyday life transferred to the stage. There is no such thing as an accident for its own sake. Everything is caused by the intervention of powers outside ourselves. In a drama, even in a farce, these powers create the situation that men must bear or succumb to. All the virtuosity the dramatist can deploy in guiding the course of events in the plot has only one purpose: to show the "reactions" of the characters in the story. No development in the plot is inevitable. Miracle and accident govern. Standing the tests and the unmasking of individuals are more important than progressive development of character. What actually happens is not so important as how it comes to pass. Basically, the actions of the protagonists are reactions.

In such a drama, which Marcel Carayon calls "the purest drama," the playwright can allow his imagination a free hand. The title of one of Lope's comedias, *There Could Hardly Be More Confusion*, could be used as the label for this whole category of plays. The attention of the audience is fixed not on the conclusion but on the unraveling of the entanglements. These entanglements can take on the most fantastic and impossible shapes, however realistic the point of departure might have been. At bottom, the realism of the cloak-and-sword comedia is only an appearance of reality. It is only a staged reality, as the drama theorists of recent centuries were to discover only after much toilsome research. Naturalism cannot be art because the simple reproduction of nature is not a spiritual creation. Nature and art are not harmonizing as components of the real universe but are diverging.

While Lope and his contemporaries demanded that the artist take nature as his model, they advocated not merely a slavish counterfeit, but a raising of the model to greater heights as a type, a transforming of the elemental into the human.

Real life was only the raw material out of which the artist molded his own reality. In order to convert this raw material into the imaginary life of the theater, the artist called his imagination into play. There are no bounds to the imagination. This aesthetic truism is to a high degree in accordance with the Spanish outlook on life, for which reality in a material sense did not exist. Tirso de Molina says: "The probable and the improbable, what we see with our eyes open—is it more confirmed than is a phantom? What is and what is not, alas, we really do not know. Life's possibilities far surpass our perception and our understanding." In the realm of the spirit Spaniards believe in no recognizable logic. Therefore it betrays total ignorance of the mental attitude of the Spaniard to accuse Spanish comedia of lacking psychological justification. The exercise of psychology was never intended or desired. It is hardly likely that many of the onlookers had given thought to such questions. The enchanting effect of the fantastic adventures on the stage was not conducive to reflection.

We know that Alonso de la Vega, a pupil of Lope de Rueda, was the last Spanish baroque dramatist to write his plays in prose. After him verse drama was the rule. Writing in verse must have seemed as natural to Lope de Vega as it did to Ovid, who was said to have spoken often in verse even in his daily life. Even Lope's theoretical writings are composed in verse.

As late as 1590 the scholar Alonso López Pinciano stated: "Drama loses its charm when not written in verse form, even though it may gain in veracity." It is difficult for a non-Spaniard to understand the dramatic effectiveness of changing the meter. It would be completely misguided to be so faithful to the original text as to use these meters in translations. Lope was a composer in his own language. Vossler correctly asserted that some of Lope's comedias cry out to be set to music so their full beauty and expressiveness can be realized. Lope's verse forms go back to both old Spanish and contemporary Italian sources. He mastered the possibilities of both, recognizing their usefulnes for the theater.

Lope's dialogue alternates between the Spanish short line, the redondilla (an octosyllabic quatrain), the quintilla (a five-line octosyllabic strophe), and such passages, and the more sophisticated Italian long line for sextets, octaves, sonnets, and the like. But he also learned and mastered the unrhymed antique measure and knew how to apply it correctly where appropriate. With his increasing maturity he became more rigorous in manipulating these forms. He himself wrote about them in *The New Art of Writing Plays*:

> Ten-meter lines are good for complaints.
> Sonnet form is suitable to express expectation.
> Reports are best imparted in romance form
> But romances are even more impressive in octaves.
> Serious worthy subjects should be in tercets
> And redondillas are for love's realm.

Farces, he says, should be spoken in phrases nearer to ordinary speech, so they demand fewer canzonets (a short, light, gay song), more redondillas. After 1610 Lope de Vega's preference for the authentic Spanish verse forms increased. His gradual concentration on Spanish popular forms of expression is revealed in his more frequent use of assonance as used in the romance and in his decreasing use of Italian forms.

A much more rewarding subject for the non-Spanish reader is Lope's characterizations, as it was through him that these became stock types in the baroque theater.

5. *The Characters of the Comedia*

In contrast to the Italian *commedia dell'arte*, which used stereotyped characters that were there from the start, Lope and his predecessors reached out avidly for life's full scope and extracted from it exactly the characters they required for a specific story. Each character in a Spanish comedia is presented as an individual. Only externally does the character seem to be a type. In Lope's later plays and those of his successors the characters were far more individualized than they were in Italian theater.

We can only begin to speak of an actual range of character types when we reach the work of Agustín Moreto y Cabaña. In his work we are offered a variety of characterizations precisely because in it the protagonists are given roles decisive for the accomplishment of Moreto's objectives. For to his audiences, the suspense of a comedy of character arises from the questions: How does the avaricious hero, the hypocritically sanctimonious one, the arriviste, and others, arrive at his goal? Why does psychological makeup not prevent him from reaching it?

In the early Spanish comedia the problem was differently stated. It was not "how does the hero attain his aim?" Rather it was, "how does he overcome the obstacles that stand in his way?" In the situation comedy the character, informed at the beginning, is shaped by the sum of the attitudes he takes in a variety of circumstances. It is only through these responses that he can be labeled.

In the comedy of character, however, the character is established as a type at the beginning of the play. What is of deciding importance is how man as a type reacts. If he decides to act contrary to his makeup, if he conquers and overcomes himself (a requirement of great drama, but not of great comedy), then he can diverge from the stock type of the early Spanish theater and rise above his type into an individual hero. Neither Molière's classical form of comedy nor the Italian *commedia dell'arte* ever contemplated such a development. In them the characters never change.

Lope was the first to cast persons as types, but it was the late Moreto who first began consciously to make use of them, even if he did so in a much freer form than did the dramatists in other Mediterranean countries.

Pairs of lovers stand in the center of the cloak-and-sword comedias. There is the cavalier and his lady, the manservant and the lady's maid. Up to that point we cannot yet speak of any specifically Spanish cast of characters. These two pairs of stock characters belong in the realm of international comedy. Any individuality they may possess is not inherent in the roles themselves. It lies in the uniqueness of the dramatist's conception of them. The Italian, and even more the French comedy, finds these pairs of lovers essential to the plot. In French and Italian comedy the noble pair of lovers are pictured very conventionally. The man is elegant, ardent, noble. The woman is innocent, enraptured, passionate. In Molière's lovers we cannot yet detect individual traits in his stereotyped characters. The roles are boring, tiresome. Even a good actor can do little with them.

There are similar roles in the Spanish comedias, but they are with far more individuality. In the French comedias, the same characters, such, for instance, as the leading lover, must always act the same when confronted with the same situation. Not so with the Spanish protagonist. The latter is first of all an individual. Only after that is he faithful to his assigned role in the plot. The qualities that are essential to defining his character are qualities that define him as a cavalier in the real world, such as *nobleza* (nobility of bearing), and above all, his devotion to honor.

The most significant of his motives is love. Although this love is never spiritualized, and although the erotic gallant in the Spanish theater is the most characteristic, his love is basically disinterested. It is more important to him, and a more convincing proof of his love, to show he is worthy of his lady, than to possess her. In this respect also, the supremacy of the spiritual and the attitude that all being is only seeming, may have exerted the controlling influence. To be consistent, however, the self-same attitude leads also to the exactly opposite conclusion—that sins committed in the play, for love, are not regarded as sinful in the moral or theological sense, because basically they are only play with mere appearance. Only when man's honor is insulted or when the good order of the realm of the abstract is disrupted, are these amorous sins experienced as subjects of guilt.

So the gallant, whose finest qualities are *nobleza* and *generosidad*, retains the esteem of the audience even if he becomes a sinner in a moral sense. He remains the hero even when he is a seducer, while the man he betrays is either left out in the cold or succumbs in a duel.

When the audience knows that the hero's protestations of love are honest, it will set aside its moralistic censure for the sake of such emotion. It will rejoice in the success of such devotion. What the consequences may be do not interest either the dramatist or the audience. They are interested only in the hero's achievement of his goal. This is also true about the heroine. The audience finds of dramatic interest only the moment of her self-assertiveness, her revolt against convention and against the strictness of the unwanted protection in which she was confined.

The lady, the loved one, must be aristocratic, beautiful, virtuous, well-born, and must always conduct herself consistently with her character. Her part, too, must revolve around love and honor. The comedia knows practically no other motives. Even women's traditional duties, motherhood for example, never appears as a dramatic consideration. This is in keeping with the basic character of adventure in the plays, which rules out everything static or routine.

The Spanish comedia has other traditional characters. There is the selfish cavalier, who is interested only in enjoying his possessions or preferably those of the lady he is wooing. There is the demimondaine, the courtesan parading in the costume of a great lady. Both are figures well-known in the social life of the period, or if you prefer, mirror figures of the nobler protagonists.

There are also the roles of the fathers. They are always old and conservative and, according to the requirement of the plot, presented as either noble or comical. The author is not especially interested in them. Their time for adventures being decisive to their lives is long past. Other roles are usually variations on those we have named.

Let us return to the gracioso and his feminine counterpart. Those characters in the Spanish theater, in parallel with the development of theater in other countries, became little by little central to the action and tended to overshadow the others. This is consistent with audience psychology of all times and peoples. Preference for the comic tends to prevail. One might regard that as a form of decadence, but it seems that the almost magic power of the comic element has more than once saved theater from lapsing into the undramatic.

According to tradition, Bartolomé de Torres Nahárro introduced the gracioso from Italy. This generalization is negated by the presence of somewhat similar types as early as in *La Celestina* (1499) and in the plays of Juan del Encina. It becomes even more invalid when one considers the timelessness and the international ubiquity of the comic figures in world theater generally, to which the Spanish type of buffoon contributes only a few peculiar nuances. It seems then as erroneous to speak of an Italian import as to claim it as a national Spanish invention.

Though Hispanists of all eras have striven to crystallize the peculiarly Spanish qualities of the gracioso the result of their endeavors apply also, with only slight variations, to the slave characters in classical comedy, the harlequin in the Italian drama, the buffoons in German comedy, and to like characters in other theaters. If, nevertheless, a particularly Spanish type was created, this must be credited to Lope de Vega, who transformed it and gave it individuality, in contrast to the stock Italian harlequin and its cognate figures.

According to Vossler, who took great pains to analyze the characterization of the gracioso, "the device of the parallel contrast between master and servant, or noble hero and jester, is as old as the tragi-comedy form of antiquity." He attributed it specifically to Plautus, and added: "But before Lope, no dramatist knew how to utilize this two-story scaffolding so masterfully and ornamentally."

And Heinz Kindermann correctly recognized that the gracioso stands much closer to the Shakespearean fool than to the harlequin in the Italian *commedia dell'arte*. The gracioso injects parody into even a serious play. His Spanish lineage stems from the clown of the interludes, and the one-man barnstorming shows, the silly man of Juan del Encina, and the lackey of *La Celestina*. The latter already indicates the position in which he will appear on the stage in the future: as servant.

Now in the comedia we recognize again the timeless comic figure as we saw him appear when he was the slave in the works of the ancient Roman comedy writers. The type we call picaro, the cheerful rogue, the mischievous knave, was developed in the Spanish short story and given currency in the comedia. The true gracioso, as he appears in the plays of earlier Spanish dramatists, was created in actual stage experience and not out of any literary tradition.

Lope de Vega himself was in error when he asserted that the *figura del donaire* (the speaker of witticisms), the comic character, was included by him for the first time in his comedia *The Buttercup*. This play was composed by him in 1598, at a time when he was already an experienced dramatist, one accustomed to complying with the demands of actors and audiences. It can be demonstrated that he had a gracioso come on the stage in a great many of his earlier plays. Lope frequently utilized the gracioso to interrupt a serious conversation with absurdly inappropriate jokes or quotations. In these plays he is usually a poor devil of inferior status, who tries to imitate the more elegant diction of the cultivated cavaliers, but does so at a moment when it is out of place. He became a really interesting figure only when the producer needed a meaty role for some specific actor he wished to place. We know this much from Velásquez and Porres, the best-known producers of the plays of Lope de Vega. The graciosos of Lope de Vega were born out of actual theatrical practice.

The special liking of Spaniards for everything presented in contrasts shows itself in other connections. It can be seen in the practice of pairing passionate eroticism with religious asceticism or of implanting alternately pious devotion and ruthless robbery in the same character.

The typical gracioso caught up in earthly matters serves as a contrast or opposite to the hero who strives to attain sublime ideals. This contrast between master and servants begins to show itself even in the kind of language they use. The high-flown affected metaphors used by the gentlemen and ladies is contrasted by the forthright language used by the lower classes. And the presentation of contrasts is not merely superficial. It is derived from the basic attitude of the main characters toward life in general. The gracioso is the only figure in the Spanish theater who is permitted to be all that is contrary to the ideals of the time, or, to put it another way, to be the materialistic reflection of an idealistic attitude.

These gracioso figures live by their instinctual drives. To them the body is more important than mind or soul. They are always thinking about food and drink. Kindermann said of them that "Their view of life is extremely earthy. Money means more to them than honor, food more than morals, safety more than any act of heroism."

Often, it is true, they are only saying aloud what their masters conceal or must hide beneath a veneer of idealistic convention. Still, we must not allow this presentation to mislead us into supposing that the dramatist is trying by this means to convey criticism of the social customs of the day. This realistic portrait of a servant is only intended to bring out in sharper outline the grand contours of Spanish nobility and high-mindedness.

Vossler correctly named the gracioso "an offspring of the joy Spaniards take in the ambiguity of everything, in contrast and parody, in gradualism and parallelism." The eleven characteristics of the gracioso figure, which Maria Haseler enumerates, seem to be general characteristics of the comic figure in the world theater. As she advances some special qualities as well, they might be listed here briefly. They are:

(1) parody of the principal action;
(2) participation in the action by giving apparently well-meant advice, even though it may be intended to deceive; the same without taking part in the action;
(3) expressing realism, cynicism, derision;
(4) manifesting surprising cultivation, knowledge of antiquity;
(5) being forward;
(6) making facetious remarks, punning, telling funny yarns;
(7) showing boastfulness or cowardice;
(8) being critical of women;
(9) being critical of general conditions of the period;
(10) being avaricious;
(11) being greedy for food.

But the essential function of the gracioso was theatrical. He was the intermediary between the hero and the audience, the last descendant of the comedian who speaks directly to the audience, as the emcee still does in our modern cabaret shows. He was the great master of disillusionment who always showed the game up to be nothing but a game. He did this not through philosophical witticisms, but in a purely theatrical manner in the course of the action. As an extreme example: when his master is being beaten he tells him not to worry, the play will soon be over.

Thus the gracioso, which, from the origins of his

type, certainly seemed destined to become a stock character, developed instead into a highly individualized theatrical figure. In the later comedias he takes the center of the stage. In those of Agustín Moreto he is quite independent, often robbing the other parts of interest.

6. The Metaphysics of the Comedia Writers

In conclusion it would seem relevant to attempt to set forth from the great wealth of comedia literature the basic concepts prevailing at the time, which are important for the present-day critic and theatergoer. The Spanish dramatist wrote in terms of these basic concepts, without the intention of imparting a personal meaning differing from these concepts.

The comedia is to be considered the offspring of the mentality of the time in which it was created. The Spanish dramatist did not indulge in any philosophical speculations; even less did he consider theater a moral institution. The purpose of his comedias was simply to entertain, nothing more. If they have become documents of historical significance, it is due only to these basic concepts, not to his individual world view.

Spanish stage compositions of the seventeenth century represent more than just a residue of that collective mentality out of which the epic poetry of the Middle Ages was born. It was precisely that collective mentality of the Middle Ages that evoked a reblooming in Spain of the seventeenth century, while in all the rest of Europe quite different cultural developments were taking place.

God does not act, he lets things happen. His presence is undramatic, as is all else that is permanent.

Life itself is inscrutable. Chance and marvel rule it. The way man masters vicissitudes, which range from the most trivial daily experience to the most exalting metaphysical encounter—this to the Spaniard is the dramatic element. There is no ultimate hopelessness. The Spanish dramatists never lead us much away from good order, for the Spaniards are always in full possession of a sense of good order that they can never lose. They do not have the fear of the unknown. Even the most perilous adventure becomes an expression of their affirmation of life.

In the shadow of this sense of good order, of which the most recognizable symbol is the ever-present awareness of death, they comprehend all of this life as semblance and illusion. For us it remains an almost impenetrable paradox that this consciousness of illusion at the same time creates as much joy as the illusion itself. The visible incarnation of this basic concept is the play on the stage. With it, the Spaniard "found a format in which the concept of human life as all semblance and illusion became a visible and ever-present symbol" (Werner Brüggermann). Francisco Quevedo, a contemporary of Lope de Vega, expressed it thus:

> Never forget that life is but a play,
> And all this world is nothing but a farce.
> The scenes change in a twinkling
> And we are all no more than actors in it.
> Never forget that God ordained the play
> And organized its wide-ranging plot
> Into such acts as he chose to invent.
> And handed out the parts and roles
> And that the length and depth of all the action
> Lie in the hands of that unique playwright.

And "somehow or other," said Vossler,

> The beyond looms over the most worldly,
> thoughtless, gayest play. Even in the cloak-and-
> sword comedia, in which sheer high spirits and
> joy of life operate, there is something beyond the
> individual participant. If it is not a pious belief
> in the church, it is a national, earthy sense of
> social honor suitable to the rank of the hero.
> Belief and honor are the bases along which all
> worthwhile acts and purposes are conducted in
> this sometimes splendid, sometimes barren, some-
> times insignificant, sometimes spectacle-filled
> Spanish stage. Every single actor on it represents
> in part his nation and his church. Each one
> represents something more than himself.

It was from that point of view that the fashion of
writing for the stage derived its metaphysical founda-
tion. It would have been unthinkable otherwise in that
century in Spain. What was real was the certainty of
death and judgment. It was this certainty that compelled one to penance and self-denial. Theater was
escape out of this reality into the mirage of pulsating
life.

Although we know from his own words that Lope
aimed at nothing more in his comedias than a reflection
of daily life true to nature, we must not forget that this
Lope was, at the same time, a gallant seeker after
adventure and a priest. Even his "true to nature"
renderings were for him only a rendering of the
appearance, the illusion, of this world, no matter how
intoxicating they may have been for him and for his
audience. "Lope's stagecraft unfolds with an unreflect-
ing instinct for the theatrical and the histrionic, that

mysteriously also corresponds to a cosmic sense of the transitoriness, the illusory quality, and the insignificance of all things mortal" (Erwin Laaths).

No reference to present time or to current reality ever lost their relevancy to the next world. Even what was tied to time and place was oriented toward universals. The aim of every plot was to lead the thinking back to undisturbed harmony. Human and divine elements were always presented on their separate levels in hierarchical order. It is for this reason that the Spaniard does not truly know what tragedy is. Everything leads only to a higher order. At the least there is always a rhetorical flourish at the end to signal that things have taken a turn for the better.

The plot itself was life as an adventure. But the determinant of the action is not human will but fate that must be overcome. Love is also of interest as action because it must overcome obstacles. Heroes must conquer life, not shape it. Their alternatives are to persevere and hold out or to react to the challenge swiftly. Otherwise they are uninteresting dramatically.

Characteristically, Tirso de Molina calls despair a vice of faintheartedness. Nor do the figures on the stage know melancholy. At most it is a passing mood, an arabesque.

In the early comedias women endured only by suffering. The jealous woman in Lope's work, even if deceived, appears as a comical figure in contrast to her appearance in the work of all other dramatists of other periods. In Lope's dramas she does not pass the test because she cannot endure. It was in the work of Tirso de Molina that they too first began to fight.

The adventure of life knows love and jealousy, honor and the injury to honor, God and Satan. But even stranger to the heroes of the Spanish stage than faintheartedness and despair are abnormalities, as they cannot be part of any good order. Such evils as homosexuality and incest are synonymous with heresy. It is only madness, real or pretended, that can be shown on the stage. The Spanish comedia shunned everything negative and completely abandoned itself to the acceptance of life.

Corresponding to the Mediterranean temperament, the basic theatrical element was contrast. The dramatic effect of contrast may have developed as a consequence of Spain's history. Spain was divided between believers and unbelievers, between Spaniards and Moors. It was divided between the luxury of the court and the misery of the masses, the magnificence of the cathedrals and the wretchedness of the peasant huts. The paradox of the differing concepts of honor sprang from the contradiction between the aristocratic and the religious interpretation of honor.

Yet all these antithetical elements were real only on the stage. In actual life they were not opposed to one another but step by step formed the structure of a world that to us moderns appears unjust and inconceivable. Even the much discussed contrast between profane and mystical love was, at bottom, only apparent. Tirso de Molina, that wisest of Spanish dramatists, was the first to recognize their common origin. Vossler said:

> Tirso's poetry is full of echoes of contrasts between profane and mystical affection. I do not know of another writer for the Spanish stage who was so continuously occupied with, and so irresistably attracted by, the inwardness of the human soul,

with what we today call the unconscious, or the subconscious, or the suppressed feelings we banish from daylight.

The love that was always the subject of cloak-and-sword comedias was always sensual and carnal. The professed idealism of the cavalier was, however, not unmasked as hypocrisy. Basically the Spaniard felt no direct contrasts, however effectively he saw them portrayed on the stage, between the duality of ideas. To him everything was semblance, unreality, illusion, opacity, the ultimate things.

Therefore we can identify three basic attributes of Spanish comedia:

(1) The conscious illusion, which can be destroyed at any time, as it is founded on pretense, not on reality. The actor who steps out of his role at the end of every play in order to take leave of his audience was at that time unthinkable in the theater of other nations.

(2) The primacy of situation over action. It is of little consequence what the principals do. How they do it, how they react to the given situation, is vital.

(3) The unlimited dominance of fantasy, an aspect no classical dramatist would acknowledge. It is the offspring of the Catholic belief in miracles and of the Spanish love of adventure. Jorge Toledano says of this: "This is the true art of Spain, to which the real world is too limiting."

It is with Moreto that a new basic concept first won recognition. The French influence became perceptible. The stricter rules of playwriting were only the outward symbol of an inner change. The old values, especially honor, no longer played the leading roles. Inner developments became more important than outward ones. A tendency toward the freedom of the individual to make decisions was discernible. "Before the time of Moreto, the individual is the object of the dramatic process but in Moreto's work he is its subject" (Uwe Bennholdt-Thomsen). But the writer did not yet demand complete freedom of human consciousness for its own sake, but only for the realization of a superior idea.

For us today it is difficult to grasp the thought that a dramatic art so completely spiritual even in its cheapest forms was regarded by its practitioners as only a poetic sideline, or as a way of making money, or as an avocation. They all, with few exceptions, dealt with it in the terms expressed by Lope de Vega when he has the king say to the dramatist in his comedia *The Prince of Illescas*: "Try to please the people and you will be on the right road." And Cubillo added the admonition: "Nothing unpleasant on the stage!" The exclusion of all unpleasant political allusions was easy to understand. The rule followed was to please the king and the people. Two centuries of literary theater and half a century of political theater makes this attitude appear to us dull and inartistic.

We can perhaps recognize in this very limitation as to what was essentially theatrical and entertaining the reason Spanish comedia marks a high point in the history of the European stage. It had no purpose other than to be itself. It preached neither morals nor propaganda. It did not try to cultivate or educate. It wished only to play, to make believe. In addition, the combination of antithetical forms of dramatic intensity with epic elements and with lyrical-musical accompaniment was not a mere aesthetic experiment, but a reflection of the feeling that contrasts signify not disintegration but represent constructive elements.

7. *The Legacy of the Comedia*

An abrupt decline of the Spanish theater set in with the death of Philip IV (1665). This must be ascribed not only to inner disintegration but also to external events. Clerical attacks on the immorality of the theater began to increase and did not stop even when confronted with the works of Calderón. Velásquez, the chronicler of the Spanish theater, named Lope de Vega as *el primer corrempedor* (the first corrupter) of the Spanish stage. He was exceeded only by Calderón, whom Velásquez described as a seducer to evil. As happens so frequently in intellectual history, there is a paradoxical alliance between antagonistic movements when they join forces to attack a third. The Spanish theater succumbed to the combined superior strength of clerical severity and rejection by followers of the Enlightenment. The influence of French classicism became gradually stronger. The Spanish comedia was rejected as naive and barbarous, and the works of the golden age sank into oblivion.

More than a century later, a national consciousness newly awakened after the Napoleonic Wars led to a new recognition of the greatness of the comedias. Spain came to this awareness of its theatrical wealth through the appreciation of non-Spaniards such as the Schlegel brothers, Lord Byron, Victor Hugo, and Chateaubriand. Juan Eugenio Hartzenbusch is credited with having reawakened the interest in the old comedias in their native land. Both nationalistic and religious tendencies seem to have acted in favor of the literature of the golden age rather than a real appreciation of the eminent value of the comedias.

Whatever the fate of the comedia within Spain, its

material remained beloved as themes for non-Spanish dramatists. It would be unjust to speak of plagarism. We know that the Spanish dramatists borrowed prodigally from each other. Not fewer than four comedias by Moreto are derived from comedias by Lope de Vega. One of these is his renowned *Answer Scorn with Scorn*, which was modeled on Lope's *The Ugly Beauty*.

The earliest evidence of Spanish influence was noted in Italy. Spanish comedias have been important there since 1620. Carlo Gozzi repeatedly adapted plays by Moreto.

The direct influence of the comedias was most strongly experienced in France, in spite of the fact that the strongest countermovement existed there. An effort was made to psychologize the comedias. It was the greatest dramatists who were most strongly drawn to them. Corneille's *Consequences of a Lie* was adapted from Lope de Vega's *Loving Not Knowing Whom*, his *Don Sanche d'Aragon*, from Lope's *The Palace Disordered*. Molière's *Amorous Doctor* was derived from Lope's *Waters of Madrid*; his *Learned Ladies*, from *Belisa's Pruderies*. Jean de Rotrou, Thomas Corneille, Paul Scarron, and Philippe Quinault also made adaptations of Spanish comedias. Rotrou especially became a conscious imitator of Spanish comedias.

In England the Spanish comedia only began to become influential after the decline of the great Elizabethan and Jacobean dramatists. It is not certain that Shakespeare knew Lope's works, or that Lope knew Shakespeare's, but both probably drew ideas from the same sources. Lope worked the same materials Shakespeare did in *Romeo and Juliet*, *Cymbeline*, *A Winter's Tale*, *As You Like It*, and *All's Well that Ends Well*.

Much Ado about Nothing is probably drawn from the same source as Moreto's *Answer Scorn with Scorn*. John Fletcher's *Maid in the Mill* seems to be a conscious adaptation of the theme we find in Lope's *Temptation of Helen*. *La Celestina* had been translated into English by James Mabbe as early as 1631. John Dryden was the first English dramatist to adopt a comedia for the English stage.

Ludvig Holbert, who is regarded as the founder of Danish literature, wrote *A Trip to the Well*, an adaptation of Lope de Vega's *Waters of Madrid*.

The Spanish comedia became known in Germany through performances by barnstorming comedians, if we accept the *Celestina*, which had already been offered in Germany in 1520, and by way of the Dutch and Italian stage.

The plays first became of interest from a literary point of view, in Lessing's time. He often referred to them in his *Hamburg Dramaturgy*, and to the fact that the Spaniards had just then come into fashion in Germany. "Rarely does a trader from Hamburg return from Cadiz if he had made a good profit there, without bringing along a couple of comedias with him." But still, a knowledge of Spanish literature seems to have been rather vague. A sentence in the *Theory of Poesy* by Christian Heinrich Schmid, which appeared in 1767, sounds odd to us. He says: "The Spaniards have some kinship with the Chinese because of their love of adventure. Love of the supernatural is preserved among them because of their Moorish inheritance."

Goethe showed better understanding of Spanish dramaturgy, not only by his preference for Calderón (he was the first to recognize him as an intellectual poet) but also by the influence of the cloak-and-sword comedia in his own work. He himself wrote in his

Poetry and Truth, about his singspiel *Claudine of Villa Bella*, that the play probably originated at a time in his life when he "was endeavoring to work up romantic subjects different from the journeyman operas, and considered that a combination of noble concepts with frivolous action would be a good idea for the stage, something new to us at the time, but not at all unusual with the Spanish writers."

To have succeeded in establishing Spanish comedia in Germany is an accomplishment of the romantics, principally August Wilhelm Schlegel and Ludwig Tieck, even if they interpreted the Spanish spirit in their own terms. Franz Grillparzer is to be credited with having fully recognized the significance of Lope de Vega without interpreting him romantically. However little his adaptations of Lope's *King Ottokar* and *The Jewess of Toledo* resemble the originals, his studies of Lope that extended over four decades clearly testify to his appreciation of Lope's special genius.

One interesting facet of the theatrical history of the comedia is commented upon by Mary Austin in "Folk Plays of the Southwest," *Theater Arts*, August 1933:

> It has never been sufficiently emphasized that the period of the *entrada* of Spain in the territory of what is now the United States was also the period of Spain's distinguished flowering in the drama. All the time that exploration and settlement was being made north of the Rio Grande, Lope de Rueda, Cervantes, Lope de Vega and Calderón were producing their scores of comedias, *autos*, *pasos* and *entreméses*, and the interest in the writing of drama was such that the king and the common man equally participated in it. . . . And this was an interest which traveled with the Con-

quistadores into New Spain, so that the first
company of settlers who ventured there, sat down
on the banks of the Rio Grande when they reached
it, nothing daunted by their incredible sea voyage
and the additional four months on horseback, and
performed a play of their progress written by one
Captain Farfan, good-naturedly spoofing their
adventure. It is always one of the thrilling expecta-
tions of searchers of records of that time, that one
may yet come on a copy of that earliest American
drama.

As for the second dramatic production of New
Mexico, we did come upon the manuscript no
longer than half a dozen years ago not ten miles
from the place in which it was first produced
July 10, 1598, in the plaza at San Juan Pueblo,
while the Indians sat stolidly on the housetops, not
being yet certain that the horses from whose backs
the lines were spoken, would not eat them. This
was in celebration of the founding of the capital
of the new province, under Oñate. The play in
question was a drama of the Moors and the
Christians, performed entirely on horseback,
which seems to have followed the Spanish army
around the world. I have traced it at Havana de
Cuba, at British Guiana, in the Philippines, in
California, and any number of versions of it in
Mexico. But in all these the purest version appears
to be that one which is still performed occasionally on Holy Cross Day in the vicinity of San
Juan, where it is still done on horseback, with the
traditional business. In Mexico, owing to the
prejudice against allowing a free use of horses to
the natives, it degenerates into a dance, with sword
play and music. But at Alcade and Santa Cruz,
New Mexico, although the text has been corrupted
by being handed down these three hundred and
thirty-odd years largely by word of mouth and

occasional transcriptions by unlettered hands, it is still possible to make out a tolerable version of the dialogue, and the business appears scarcely to have suffered at all.

Who composed the drama of *Los Moros y los Cristianos* there is no knowing. Cervantes, in his account of the Teatro de Corrales, explicitly stated that in his youth there were no plays of the Moors and the Christians to give zest to their remembered performances, which would put the writing of this one at least as late as the 70's or 80's of fifteen hundred.

Modern productions of the comedias will be discussed in the chapters on individual writers and as part of the review of individual plays.

8. La Celestina

No study of the comedia would be complete without mention of *La Celestina*, a literary masterpiece that exercised a long-lasting influence on Spanish theater and fiction. *Celestina*, a work in twenty-one acts, appeared in 1499 and showed the literary components of the developing Spanish theater. It was a mixture of epic and drama that proved decisive for the direction subsequently taken by the comedia writers. Generally speaking, just about all the elements of the later Spanish comedia are present in this dramatic epic, including the motifs of the cloak-and-sword comedia and the comedy of manners, the contrast between earthy and more ideal love, parody and irony, the type of *lacayo* (servant) out of which the jesting gracioso emerged, and the special form of the *coplas*, the scenic couplets, the topical songs. By 1520, *La Celestina* was being translated into German, and by 1630 into English. Although it was intended only for reading, it became the single most active stimulant to the dramas of Spain's golden age.

Just about all theater historians rate this composition the most enigmatic in theater history. Is it a novel in dialogue or an epic drama? It affected not only the development of Spanish drama as his other work did, but it was never intended by its authors for stage presentation. Lope de Vega's effort to imitate it miscarried.

The reasons that led to its unusual literary form seem quite clear: in the Arab world any theatrical presentation of gods and men was prohibited. There was no Spanish theater until the final liberation of Spain from the Moors, so the dramatic gift was compelled to seek outlets other than the theater. Direct discourse in the novel became ever more predominating until dialogue burst through the confines of the narrative form. To assign the origin of this first European form of epic theater to the religious drama of the stations of the cross in the Middle Ages seems hardly plausible as Spaniards of that time consistently regarded *La Celestina* as a novel. Lope de Vega's *Dorotea*, which followed the format of the *Celestina*, was similarly never meant for the stage. Nevertheless, the illustrations in the published book clearly indicated its theatrical possibilities. They show little huts with big gates, such as we know from other contemporary stage settings. There are towerlike structures that can be considered models for the background scenery of the later Spanish stage.

La Celestina, or *Comedia de Calisto y Melibea*, is written in prose and appeared anonymously. The question of authorship is still disputed. The first edition came out in Burgos in 1499. It consists of sixteen acts. By the 1502 edition it had grown to twenty-one acts. By 1526 the work had grown to twenty-two acts. We believe the writer of the first act was either Rodrigo de Cota or Juan de Mena. The other acts were probably by Fernando de Rojas, who is said to have been a converted Jew from the neighborhood of Toledo. He lived from 1475 to 1537. The work appeared in Italian in Venice about sixteen years after it was first published. In 1520 Christoff Wirsung in Augsburg dedicated his German version to Matthew Lang, archbishop of Salzburg. French and English editions followed soon after. The anonymity of the Spanish original might have been due to fear of the Inquisition, and this may also account for the introduction by the author, in which he emphasizes the moral impact of the work as "a wholesome pill in a sugar coating." The vices it describes, and also the passions of love, are meant to deter youth from following the same path.

The subject is not original. More than a century earlier, Juan Ruiz de Hita had used a similar motif in his *Pamphilus* (an episode in *The Book of Good Love*). There too, a crafty woman go-between acts as intermediary between a noble lover and his loved one. We find variations of this theme in all the narratives of the Middle Ages as well as in Roman comedy, which we might do well to regard as the original source of the theme.

But the author or authors of *La Celestina* were the first to portray the two lovers and their matchmaker with such art that they became permanent fixtures in world literature. Calisto and Melibea are accurately called the first pair of classical lovers in the European theater. Eros had the unnamed principal role in the work. He triumphs in the end over death in spite of all the suffering he himself has caused.

Moritz Rapp states that in spite of his full appreciation of the true-to-life qualities of this work "it is utterly without any dramatic interest." He may be right that its authors had no dramatic purpose in mind in writing the work, but he is mistaken in not calling attention at the same time to the brilliant format of its structure, which admittedly contradicts all the accepted rules of dramatic construction. As for Heinz Kindermann's comment that the worth and merit of the work lie in its lively picture of humanity rather than in its moral or dramatic elements, it is my view that he appraised the dramatic features too much like a stepmother. It is hardly possible to advance a theoretical definition or explanation of this brilliant literary structure when its obvious succession of engrossing dramatic and playful lyrical scenes points to a specific technique that the Spanish dramatists were able later to apply with such success.

La Celestina is no simple group of sequential scenes, but a very intentionally, though perhaps unconsciously created, series of perceptive insights into the fate of a group of people. The dramatic tension it produces is so potent that it keeps one's interest constantly alive throughout the depicted scenes.

The greatly appreciated quality of the individual roles must not mislead one into thinking we see in it an early example of a drama of character. It is not the development of character that it demonstrates, but the bearing of the protagonists, their reactions to given situations. This work is also ruled by chance and miracle. Love itself is the greatest miracle, often the result of chance.

In the first scene, Calisto, pursuing his falcon, comes

into Melibea's garden. This opening is one of the most touching scenes in all world theater.

> CALISTO: Now I realize how great the Lord God is!
> MELIBEA: Why?
> CALISTO: Because he grants me the grace to drink in the sight of your beauty.

Melibea sends him away. Her severely moral up-bringing will not allow her to respond in any other way. Calisto is inconsolable and seems to despair. His manservant, Sempronio, is a devil-may-care fellow with a sense of humor, but he is not yet the sympa-thetic gracioso of the later comedias. He obtains for Calisto the aid of a procurer, the scheming Celestina. It is an immense accomplishment of the writer of this work to make this woman not only the chief character of the work but actually its heroine, as there is no kind of iniquity that is beyond her. She is an angel of the underworld, madame, witch, a fox in her cunning, queen of every wickedness.

But Celestina is only relatively wicked. She is a solicitous housemother to her prostitutes. To Calisto she is a light in his despair, a resurrection from death. She herself sees nothing reprehensible in her profession, whether she prescribes medicinal herbs, patches up a lost virginity, or arranges to couple up a pair of lovers. To her it is all a service to life, which, old as she is, she still adores with boundless affection. If she happens to be a witch who makes a pact with the god of the netherworld, it only lifts her, in one sense, to mythic greatness. At the same time this characterization seems to amount to a concession to the prevalent public opinion that matchmakers and their ilk must be in alliance with the devil himself. The true flaw in her character is her overweening greed for money. She herself does not understand why she is so obsessed by her passion for gold. She gets no personal gratification out of it. She dresses in rags. It is this vice that leads to her undoing and downfall, not her love potions, not her procuring, not her witchcraft.

She is brought to Calisto and promises to help him— for a generous payment of course. Sempronio plans to share it with her. Celestina, disguised as a vendor of yarns, gets herself into Melibea's home. By chance it is at a time when Melibea's mother is leaving on a journey. Celestina takes advantage of the opportunity to inform Melibea that Calisto is wasting away and suffering. Melibea is outraged. She wants to have Celestina thrown out of the house. Then Celestina changes her story. She says now it is only Calisto's toothache she wishes to cure. She asks Melibea to lend her Melibea's belt for this purpose, as it has many consecrated relics attached to it. Melibea does not wish to act unsympathetically. She allows herself to indulge the attraction she feels for Calisto but is concealing under a show of anger. She hands her belt over to the old woman, who knows full well that with it she can intensify Calisto's passion and extract more money from him than if she had succeeded in arranging a meeting for him.

While she is at it, she pairs off Calisto's younger valet Parmeno with Areusa, a girl in her house, though Areusa wished to remain true to her lover, who has gone off to the wars. By doing so, Celestina is protecting herself because Parmeno has hinted he might warn his master against her. The assignation she arranges in Areusa's bedroom is one of the most daringly erotic scenes in world literature.

On this, Sempronio and Parmeno and their sweethearts celebrate in Celestina's house. This is an orgy, a mixture of sex and quarreling, gluttony and lust. Old Celestina presides, though she gets no joy from anything but the wine, a substitute for the previous pleasures of love. In the midst of this scene, Melibea's servant arrives. Melibea wishes Celestina to come to her at once. She can no longer restrain her own desire. She confesses her love for Calisto. She will await her beloved at the gate of her garden.

Calisto arrives, followed by his armed servants. The two lovers speak to each other through the grating of the gate, a device we shall encounter later in countless cloak-and-sword comedias.

But a noise that sounds like the approach of the watch detail is heard. The servants run away. Calisto himself withdraws, promising to return the following night. Sempronio and Parmeno betake themselves to Celestina and demand their share of the payment. Celestina refuses to give them any money. They stab her. Calling out for a confessor, Celestina dies. The prostitute Elicia throws herself on her, calling out: "She was my mother, my benefactress!" Nevertheless, she opens the window and tries to help the assassins get away, as the watch are already knocking at the door. It is too late. The servants are captured and executed at once.

This harrowing scene is followed by one in Calisto's home. The lover is singing and accompanying himself on the lute. He is told all that has happened. But his love is greater than his distress. He goes to Melibea, and at last they are in each other's arms. Meanwhile the two women Elicia and Areusa have persuaded another lover to kill Calisto, thus avenging the death of Celestina and the servants. But this lover is a coward (and possibly a precursor for a later gracioso). He persuades still another to do it, who is equally reluctant to commit an actual murder. He only intends to make a row. Knowing that Calisto is with Melibea, with two servants standing guard, he invades the scene of love. Trying to escape, Calisto gets on a ladder. Falling off it, he plunges to his death. Melibea climbs to the tower of the house and plunges down from the top, wishing to be united with her lover in death. Her father speaks the closing words: "My gray hairs, my honor, my wealth—what are they without thee?"

It seems mistaken to see in this work only a description of the mores of the time, as more recent literary historians have tried to assert. The writers obviously concerned themselves with what to them was timelessly human. It is true that the two lovers and Celestina, as types, are eternal figures in world literature, and there is always need for a Celestina.

On one occasion Celestina says:

> But did not enough men show me respect for the sake of my girls? And did I not entertain nobles, old and young, the religious of all ranks from bishop to sacristan? Whenever I entered a church they all tore off their caps as if I were a duchess. Who had the least to do with me did himself the least good. They abandoned their prayers when they saw me coming half a mile away in order to get close enough to me singly or in pairs, to ask my wishes and to inquire about my girls. My entrance confused them so that not one of them knew what he was doing or saying. One would address me as madame, another as madrona, a third as his sweetheart, a fourth as your grace. They made arrangements about coming to my place or having me bring the girls to their homes. They

offered me cash or gifts to kiss the corner of my cloak if not my face, to wheedle me into a good mood. Now my good fortune has brought me so far that they say to me: "I hope your shoes are comfortable!"

Celestina and her world not only come up to that of Shakespeare's but go beyond his world in her description of the foibles of humanity all too human.

La Celestina is the prototype of the cloak-and-sword comedias with their mysterious trysts, their duels, their languishing lute lyrics, and their assignations in idyllic hidden parks, as well as the *comedias de teatro* of the later Spanish dramatists. Ferdinand Wolf, in calling Celestina the mother of the Spanish drama, said quite accurately: "Yes, I do not hesitate to deem it good fortune that national Spanish drama had such a mother. Let the rulebound esthetes turn up their aristocratic noses at Celestina's misbehavior and straitlaced moralizers about her immorality."

For two centuries the work has been internationally successful as a reading drama. It is to our own century that we must be grateful for the discovery that it is suitable for the stage. The most vivid translation and adaptation seems to have been implemented by the Italian Carlo Terron, though he shaped it more into a vehicle for social criticism than is likely to have been in the minds of its authors. The best-known French translation is by Marcel Achard. The most recent German translations are those by Alfred Wolfenstein, Eugen Ortner, Richard Zoozmann, Anton Rothbauer, and Christoff Eich.

There has been no lack of translations and adaptations of this unusual dialogue novel. But the year when the first effort to produce it on the Spanish stage was made remains uncertain. Outside of Spain, the effort to present it on the stage in an abbreviated and concentrated version was first made in the twentieth century. Though the work seems predestined for the German expressionistic theater between the two world wars, the experiment made by Richard Weickert in Frankfurt in the late 1920s was received with scant interest, so *La Celestina* seemed as unamenable to stage production as ever. Its adapters continued to express partiality for it, but the practitioners of the stage shied away from it.

The play remains in the permanent repertory of Spain. Luis Escoba staged it in 1957 in the Teatro Eslava in Madrid. One of his innovations was to use scaffolding to present several scenes simultaneously to avoid the need for numerous scene changes. This production had, in spite of its importance, no impact outside of Spain.

Skillful translations and adaptations often remained unproduced for a long time. Or when used, as they were in Oldenburg and Nurnberg after World War II, they received only limited response. It was Carlo Terron's production of his own adaptation in Milan in 1966 that first proved that a production of *La Celestina* could succeed and, indeed, could be more than a success, a notable event. Then hymns of praise, until then withheld by the legion of theoretical theater historians, were freely bestowed on the work as one of the most effective in world literature. Terron's *Celestina* continued to flourish as a play in Milan, where the magic-demonic background of the original was preserved.

Soon after Terron's success, Karl Paryla staged a similar version in Cologne. This production was

received by theatergoers with enthusiasm and was regarded as noteworthy by almost everybody. The
Cologne company brought its production to Berlin in
1967, where it was rated one of the best in theater
events of the season.

That a dyed-in-the-wool comic spirit such as Karl
Paryla would seize hold of this work primarily from
its comic aspect was easily foreseeable. This is not in
the spirit of the robust realism of this work, but it
did please the taste of contemporary theatergoers who
demand a frankly sensuous theater without restraints.
It is equally clear that Paryla was concerned above all
with emphasizing the social aspect of the work and
ignoring its suprarational element. The result was a
production of frankly unrestrained comic indulgence,
sobered only by a bias of social criticism.

The tower scene at the close of the play is generally
cited as the climax of the graphic images that embody
interpretation of the play. Melibea dashes upon a
spiral staircase, that is, she runs in a circle along a
revolving balustrade while a canvas backdrop in the
background slides away from her. After her leap the
balustrade and the backdrop vanish, and she lies alone
on the floor of the stage. In this production the costuming was authentic. The musical score mixed striking folkloristic tones with hard modernistic sounds.

Grete Wurm as Celestina stole the show. What
Paryla had in mind in his production was fully recognized in the reviews by almost all the commentators
who wrote of the kinship between Celestina and
Mother Courage in Brecht's play. Paryla suppressed
all mythic elements from her characterization, though
in the original she is labeled not only as a go-between
matchmaker and seamstress but also as a witch. Yet
Terron had given Celestina a big, highly realistic scene,

in which she engages in a colloquy with the devil. This could only be effective because she fully believes in the devil's existence. Paryla makes her more earthy, motherlike, though amoral, like Mother Courage. She is honest in her rogue's pride. She is equally honest in acknowledging her avarice, something she does not comprehend. To her it is beyond good and evil. This honesty renders her sympathetic to us. Even in this secularized version she remains Mother World, who rules men's proclivities, proclivities to which they are subject whether they are high or low. This was all expressed in Grete Wurm's quite matter-of-fact, almost aloof, manner of speech, in spite of, or perhaps by very reason of, her sturdy and lusty vitality. "By her creation she gave a rendering of a figure of primitive and satanic power" (Luyken).

Other critics were equally impressed. "Grete Wurm's dance of joy, her shout of triumph, when innocence comes to a fall," wrote one critic, "had something demonic in it." The theater reviewer who called Celestina "a proletarian witch" hit the bull's eye.

Parmeno was played more as an engaging, misguided young lover than as a gracioso, whereas Sempronio was played as an utter rascal from the start in spite of his coarse humor. Those who acted the lower-class roles in this game of the poor against the rich had it much easier than those who played the roles of noblemen and ladies. This was largely because of the well-staged scene of gluttony and carousal in the brothel.

Calisto and Melibea are a pair of great lovers in the classical tradition. Whether they perish because of their sin in deifying each other or because of the hopeless social order governed by different standards is quite secondary. The essential feature is that their love surmounts and survives death. But one should keep in mind that this play is no Song of Songs in praise of love.

The characters in the play are not victims of social hypocrisy. They are victims of their own passions. Celestina manipulates and directs these emotions. Princes and priests serve her as do menservants and maidservants. It is this quality that makes her into a demonic figure, and her death into tragedy. The transition from the broadly comic moods to the tragic finale is abrupt. The tragic deaths at the end are not logical, but they are ideologically necessary. The structure exemplifies the contrast technique of Spanish drama. It is the critics who saw this break as a weakness is Paryla's staging, who were making a grave error. World theater is indebted to Paryla for his achievement in making *La Celestina* into an effective theatrical event.

In other countries theater people continue with varying success in their efforts to offer *La Celestina* dramatically. It is interesting to note that as recently as February 1960 a production of *La Celestina* was banned in Mexico for what some interpreted as "reasons of morality."

In November 1960, *La Celestina* was presented in a backers' audition at the Provincetown Playhouse, in New York City. Mr. George Christopoulos called his adaptation a "hellenized" version—that is, the characters were all given Greek names—but he set the play in Tarpon Springs, Florida, about 1940.

Andres Castro directed a Spanish-language production of *La Celestina* in June 1967 at the Greenwich Mews Theater in New York City.

In the July 1969 Moscow Film Festival, director Cesar Ardavin entered his own film adaptation of this classic. After its showing at the festival the film was

hailed by *Variety* (30 July 1969) as a "very profes-
sionally made entry which rates an international
looksee." Acting, directing, sets, and photography—all
were considered superior achievements in international
film making. Director Ardavin tightly maintained suspense throughout, despite the fact that the two-hour
film was overlong for the average audience. The
characters, played by both Spanish and German actors,
were portrayed in a manner that was balanced between
realism and stagecraft.

THE WRITERS
AND THEIR COMEDIAS

An achievement so great as that of Pedro Calderón de la Barca cannot be handled within the limits of this book, the focus of which is Lope de Vega and the comedia exclusive of Calderón.* Calderón brought the cloak-and-sword comedia to new heights, imbuing it with unsurpassable poetry. Few golden-age scholars would deny that *The Phantom Lady* is the most perfect of the comedias. As for the mischievious question of which dramatist is the greater, I hold the position of Grillparzer, who, with full appreciation of Lope, rated them as equal in merit. Calderón, he wrote, was the magnificent dramatist of the comedia of manners; Lope was the magnificent delineator of the natural.

For the lover of theater, the greatness of Lope de Vega and Calderón can best be sensed by seeing them within the context of the Spanish golden age. Their precursors and contemporaries wrote plays that are masterpieces in their own right as well as being major forces in the development of the comedia.

* I hope the interested reader will want to turn to my monograph *Pedro Calderón de la Barca* in the World Dramatists Series, Frederick Ungar Publishing Co., 1973.

Juan del Encina (1469–1529)

The first important dramatist in the history of the Spanish theater is Juan del Encina. He came from the neighborhood of Salamanca, and his plays were written in the dialect of that region. He was himself an actor and, like most Spanish dramatists of his time, he was later ordained a priest. Although he spent a period of time in Rome in the service of Pope Alexander VI, I can see no Italian influence in his works. He wrote some religious pastoral poems (*eglogas*) and some mystery plays in the medieval tradition. What are of more interest are his *farsas*, a dramatic form he originated. In these, gestures are more expressive than dialogue. There is not much action in the plot, but the individual characters are powerfully drawn. By his action in Málaga, he was the first producer who linked theater operation with one of the sodalities.

Gil Vicente (1470–1536)

Encina's farces were built around little more than the comic characteristics of a few marked human types. A greater range of character types appears in the comedias of Encina's Portuguese contemporary Gil Vicente. He also wrote dialogue in his own dialect. Vicente was the first to bring a love intrigue onto the stage. He too was an actor and director. He later became dramatist at the court of Charles V.

In the midst of a tight, caste-ridden medieval society, Lope de Vega dared to write plays presenting sympathetic pictures of peasants who resisted the tyranny of villainous overlords. One of the most famous of this kind is *Fuente Ovejuna*. In this the villagers in Fuente Ovejuna unite to kill a ruthless comendador, and maintain, even under torture, that he was killed by "Fuente Ovejuna." The photograph is from a production of the Theater Arts Division of Columbia University, offered in February 1970.
THEATER ARTS DIVISION OF COLUMBIA UNIVERSITY,
NEW YORK CITY

El perro del hortelano (literally, the gardener's dog) is Lope de Vega's charming offering about a woman who is afflicted by the same failing as Aesop's dog in the manger. Countess Diana will not marry the handsome Teodoro because of his inferior social position—but she will not step aside and let her maid Marcella have him. After many scenes of intrigue and complication, amor vincit omnia— even pride and social barriers.

The popular French adaptation of this play, *Le chien du jardinier*, in a translation by Georges Neveux, has won a permanent place in French repertory theater. The play was premiered at the Théâtre Marigny in Paris in 1955. Directed by Jean-Louis Barrault, this production (opposite) starred Jean-Louis Barrault as Teodoro and Madeleine Renaud as the capricious Countess Diana.
COURTESY OF AGENCE DE PRESSE BERNAND, PARIS

In 1963, under the title *The Dog in the Manger*, this play (below) was offered by the Little Theater School of Fine Arts at Texas Christian University. The role of Diana was played by Barbara Hutson (left).
THE LITTLE THEATER SCHOOL OF FINE ARTS: TEXAS
CHRISTIAN UNIVERSITY. PHOTOGRAPH BY JAY DEE

Not So Stupid After All is Spanish comedia at its best. A seemingly effortless exhibition of dramatic writing on many levels by a master virtuoso, this play exemplifies Lope's guiding principle—to enchant his audiences. Among other things, it is a satire on literature, an allegory of the life-is-an-illusion theme, a romantic farce about the blossoming of a stupid girl when she falls in love. Critics were unanimous in extolling the acting of Käthe Braun (left), who superbly realized the flowering of a dull-witted girl into an affectionate woman, in a production at Berlin Schloßparktheater in 1956–1957, directed by Dietrich Haugk.
JLSE BUHS

Sir Miracle Comes a Cropper (opposite), by the prodigious Lope, is said to be a play that Shakespeare would have considered worthy of his pen. In this play Lope ironically and gracefully disposed of the cavalier so idealized for centuries by feudal Spain, all the while casting needle-edged barbs at the foolishness of man. An arrogant scoundrel, a selfish cad, the protagonist is called Sir Miracle by those who see him succeed through his guileful, treacherous deeds—until the day of reckoning.

The scene is from a production at the Schauspielhaus Hamburg, 1958, directed by Ulrich Erfurth, with Ulrich Haupt playing Sir Miracle.
ROSEMARIE CLAUSEN

The masterpieces of the golden age of Spanish drama could only have come into being through an intense love of theater shared by those who created it and those who watched it. The sense of being stimulated to

CALDERÓN
BY C. A. SCHWERDGEBURTH

TIRSO DE MOLINA
BY BARTOLOMÉ MAURA Y
MUNTANER

reach new heights by this nationwide passion for theater must have been felt by the four greatest dramatists of the golden age: Lope de Vega, Calderón, Cervantes, Tirso de Molina.

LOPE DE VEGA
BY F. SELMA

CERVANTES
BY THE FRENCH ARTIST
GEOFFREY

ALL REPRODUCTIONS OF
ENGRAVINGS ARE USED BY
COURTESY OF THE HISPANIC
SOCIETY OF AMERICA.

The home of the Spanish comedia for many years was the courtyards (*corrales*) of hospitals. Thus one of the great theater periods in the western world flourished in the modest setting of an open-air stage surrounded by the walls of houses. Dramas of unsurpassed greatness were presented by itinerant troupes on stages that were hastily constructed and dismantled as the need arose. In Ciudad Real the restored *corral* of Almagro (above) offers productions in the golden-age style.

The action in Vicente's plays is, more markedly than with Encina, only a pretext for showing general human failings. The concentration on the depiction of character in these plays, which seems to stem from Vicente's ignorance of the rules of dramatic composition, later became one of the cardinal principles of Spanish drama writing: it is not the plot that is important but the way the characters respond to the situation in which they find themselves.

An example of one of Gil Vicente's farces is his *Inês Pereira*, composed for a particular occasion. The plot can be briefly told. The genesis of this farce is a farce in itself. Because Vicente was not believed to have a wealth of imagination, he was given the task of writing a play on this theme: Better a mule I can depend on to carry me than a horse that throws me. *Inês Pereira* is the dramatist's answer. A young girl is wooed by a peasant who is prosperous but dull. Because of her longing for grandeur she marries instead a well-born but poor knight. He disciplines her so severely that after his early death she gladly weds the dull peasant. Not very long after, she crowns him with horns.

Bartolomé de Torres Naharro (1476–1531)

The plays of Torres Naharro stem, for the most part, from the tradition of *La Celestina*. Although Torres Naharro lived in Italy even longer than Juan del Encina did, he remained authentically Spanish in his writing. Torres Naharro classified his own comedias into definite basic types: the cloak-and-sword comedias and the comedias of situation. He was the first in Spain to structure a play. He divided his comedias into five *jornadas* (a *jornada* is a day's march). His plays are introduced by an *introito* (prologue) or an *argumento* (outline of the plot).

Beginning with him, the most important motives treated in the comedias were honor, love, and revenge. It is not certain that we can also attribute to him the precedent for the so-called mirror technique, in which the actions of the protagonists are reflected in the actions of subordinate characters or in scenes in which servants act out behavior that contrasts to the conduct of their masters. It is also uncertain whether we can credit Torres Naharro with having been the first to create the character of the gracioso.

He is more significant for us as the founder of the cloak-and-sword comedias, named for the two indispensable requisites of every Spanish cavalier. Legend tells that even the length of the cloak to be worn was prescribed by the king. The first appearance to this dramatic form can be found in Torres Naharro's comedia *Aquilana*, in which a king appears on the stage for the first time. The play is a field day for an actor, written precisely to provide what an actor would relish: a series of excellent theatrical situations, a frequent alternation between elegant love scenes that are not the slightest bit bombastic or boring and scenes of low-class revelry among the servants.

The comedia *Serafina* deals essentially with the principle of honor. But we must consider *Hymen* as the first authentic cloak-and-sword play, "with its moonlight serenades, its faint-hearted night watchmen, its raging, panting, sword-swinging rescuers of women's honor, and its ardent lovers" (Kindermann).

Torres Naharro also wrote plays of genuine social criticism. In his *Jacinta*, for example, all classes are treated alike. In his *Soldatesca* he offered a comical picture of the immoral rabble that trails after any military action. He also described the rivalries and differences between Italians and Spaniards as he had himself observed them during his life in Naples.

Although almost all his plays were banned by the Inquisition, they must certainly have been played. If not it is difficult to account for the powerful influence they exerted on the Spanish theater. It is unlikely that a bare reading of his works could have exerted such influence.

Lope de Rueda (1510–1565)

Lope de Rueda of Seville has been repeatedly named not only in his time but even today as the father of Spanish stage art. He was first a gold-leaf beater, then an actor, director, and writer. "His comedias were dialogues or eclogues between two or three shepherds and a shepherdess," wrote Cervantes in his recollections of Lope de Rueda's performances. "These little playlets were cleaned up and expanded by some interludes. Sometimes a black character, sometimes a silly peasant from Viscaya, appeared in them. Lope de Rueda himself played these parts. He did so with such cleverness and skill that one cannot imagine how anyone could have done them better."

Lope de Rueda barnstormed with his little troupe all over Spain. His wife, the singer Mariana, was the most important member besides himself. He is supposed to have performed in many noble courts as well. Four of his comedias have been preserved. They are clearly modeled along Italian lines, as, for instance,

Those Who Were Deceived, the plot of which can be traced back to the same source Shakespeare used for his *Twelfth Night, or What You Will*.

Cervantes also mentioned Lope de Rueda's interludes, short farces called *pasos*, that are far more important than his comedias. They remind one of Encina's *farsas*, but they are much more noteworthy not only because of the skill of their composition but also for their imagination. Several of them have been preserved.

Juan de Timoneda, who published Lope de Rueda's works, remarked at the close of his edition that these *pasos* could be performed during the intermissions of any play. They are quite independent of the subject of the comedias themselves. The characters in these interludes are openly of clownish nature, though their actions border on the tragic. They can be quite rightly related to the plays of Ionesco. Take, for example, the *paso* about the olive tree. A married couple are quarreling about the harvest they will reap from an olive tree they have just planted, though it will not begin to yield fruit for seven years.

Lope de Rueda earned wide recognition for his work. When he died he was accorded the honor of an elaborate public funeral in Cordoba.

His most noteworthy successors were his publisher Timoneda, Sepulveda, and Alonso de la Vega (died 1566). Vega was an actor in Lope de Rueda's troupe and was one of the last of the writers of Spanish comedias to write in prose.

Another successor was Juan de la Cueva (1550–1610), who wrote in a variety of verse forms. His intermixture of tragic and comic, elevated and ordinary, themes, had become quite commonplace by his day. He knew the rules of antiquity but consciously followed only the Spanish style.

Miguel de Cervantes Saavedra
(1547-1616)

The dramatic writings of Miguel de Cervantes Saavedra are of a character unusual to the comedia. According to his own account, he, finding himself penniless, became a writer as a means of earning a living. He had spent his early years on adventure. He had fought and been taken prisoner in North Africa, an imprisonment from which he was ransomed by his family. At first the writing of plays for the theater appeared to him to offer the easiest livelihood. Later he thought he could do better by writing stories. It was only a year before his death that he collected some of his plays for publication. This volume was far from being a complete collection because he had lost track of most of those he had written.

In writing his comedias Cervantes used as his model the tragedies of Seneca (4 B.C.–A.D. 65). Seneca was a Spanish philosopher and dramatist who spent most of his life in Rome, the capital city of the Roman Empire. In fact there was an affinity between the drama of the golden age and Seneca's drama. In both, the adventurous, the ghostly, the monstrous predominated. Seneca's theater was a theater of marvels. Cervantes was not the only Spanish comedia writer who had a predilection for it. Other dramatists, long lost sight of, were closer emulators of Seneca. One was Cristóbal Virués of Valencia.

The serious comedias of Cervantes had a direct influence on Lope de Vega's work. Lope's *La sinta siga* would never have been written without Cervantes's most famous drama, *The Siege of Numantia*. Neither would his *Algerian Captives* have been written had Cervantes's first play, *The Customs of Algeria*, not existed.

The messages of Cervantes's plays are of more consequence to us than are his observance of Seneca's formula in his comedias or his emphasis on "religious heroism," which stresses honor and immaterial advantage over possessions and victories.

These messages, addressed to the conscience of the king and of the Spanish nation, plead that the sufferings of the war prisoners in Algiers not be forgotten. Cervantes was the first comedia writer who approached the public issues of the day. He wished to be known not only as a dramatist, or a writer, or an epic poet, but as one who renders aid in time of need. Even when he was occupying himself with entertaining an audience he wished to function as an educator and wanted his heroes to be recognized as models of right conduct.

Cervantes was the first to break with the formula of the five-act play introduced by Torres Naharro. He divided his comedias into three acts. In his own mind he considered the introduction of allegorical figures on the stage his most important innovation: "I showed, or perhaps I should rather say, I was the first to bring out openly the hidden thoughts and fancies of the soul by putting allegorical figures on the stage. This was done with the general approval of my audiences and to their pleasure." Before his time, however, allegorical figures were used, certainly in religious plays if not elsewhere. But Cervantes certainly was not one to adorn himself with laurels he did not deserve. It may be that he was the first to characterize them as taking a direct part in human affairs as the guide or companion of the leading character. Or, he may not have had personal knowledge of the use of allegorical figures on the stage.

The dramas of Cervantes, which by his own account numbered thirty or so, were received by the public with enthusiasm. But his many interludes, some of which were included in the 1615 collection, are of greater interest to posterity. It is therefore strange that, so far as can be ascertained, only a single one of these valuable interludes was ever staged, while the others went only from his desk drawer to the printing press and into the reader's hands. It seems safe to assume that whatever the evidence these interludes must have been produced because they are far superior to the accomplishments of his predecessors. Indeed they exemplify the highest perfection ever achieved in this genre. Unlike the *pasos* of Lope de Rueda, whom Cervantes greatly respected, those of Cervantes do relate, more or less closely, to the comedia being presented. To be sure, this does not prevent their being performed as independent plays. Like snapshots of moments in daily life, the interludes present situations. What endows these plays with such dramatic impact are Cervantes's magnificent gift of observation and his inimitable dialogue.

However well Cervantes presents the ambiance of his time and country, almost all his plays treat themes universally comic and relevant. In *The Election of the Mayor* Cervantes dealt with the preparations for the selection of the mayor by the rural inhabitants of the area. In *The Salamanca Cave* he presents the delightful pranks of a cunning unfaithful wife who does a stylish dance, a saraband, with one of her lovers before her cheerfully feasting husband, a situation replete with superb dramatic potentiality. In *The Divorce Judge* Cervantes brings a series of ill-matched couples into court, who present incredible explanations for why they do not wish to remain married any longer. Bertolt Brecht may have borrowed the theme of this interlude for a similar scene in his *Caucasian Chalk Circle*.

In October 1966 the Teatro Español in Madrid honored Cervantes on the 350th anniversay of his death by staging two of his works. The first, the musical adaptation of the classic *Don Quixote, Man of La Mancha*, was highly approved by audience and critics alike. But Cervantes's stage play *The Siege of Numantia* received both applause and whistling—the Latin gallery's sign of displeasure. The plot of the play deals with the year-long siege of the town of Numantia by a Roman army. The women of the town, in fear of being dishonored by the Romans, refuse to allow their men to go for help. Perhaps the primary reason for the audience's displeasure is that, in twentieth-century Spain, the people, as a rule, do not like tragedies. The play had been criticized in 1602 by Lope de Vega for that very reason.

Tad Szulc, however, (*New York Times*, 5 October 1966), claimed that another reason for the play's unpopularity in present-day Spain "lies in its historical and political connotations." He wrote: "It has been produced as a rallying cry in connection with every major Spanish siege from Zaragoza in the early 19th century war of independence to the encirclement of Madrid by the Nationalists in 1937 during the civil war. As the critic of *YA* remarked today, the Madrid Republicans 'wanted to make themselves pass for Numantians.' "

Nevertheless, the production itself received enough applause to drown out most of the whistling.

The Theater of Wonders

The best-known of Cervantes's interludes, one that is still being performed, is *The Theater of Wonders*. Because of its continuing popularity and its typicality as an interlude, let us look at it.

Chanfalla, the owner of a puppet theater, and his female associate, Chirinos, arrive in a village. With them is a dwarf who provides the music. They explain to the local dignitaries who come to the square that the living tableaux they mean to present can be seen by all people except those who are new Christians, that is, converted Jews, or those born out of wedlock. Indifferent to this the dignitaries eagerly ask to see a performance on the occasion of the betrothal of the governor's daughter.

In these opening dialogues, Cervantes promptly inserted some pointed allusions to conditions well known in the village. He takes aim, for instance, at the idea of honor: "As the oak tree bears acorns, the pear tree, pears, the vine, grapes, a gentleman must produce honor. He has no choice." Cervantes also mocked the fad of writing plays for the theater. The local administrator has become a playwright. "Twenty-two comedias I have in my drawer. All new and as like each other as eggs." And he has the theater director say: "There are so many poets they obscure the sun, and they all believe they are in the fashion." He suggested too that the dramatists steal from each other.

The second scene shows the audience expectantly

awaiting the performance. This brings us again to a caustic allusion to the times. One of the men in the audience is annoyed by the dwarf musician, but the director defends the dwarf, saying: "He is a true Christian and a hidalgo, with a family name that has an excellent sound to it." To this the mayor says: "These are qualifications indispensable to a musician."

The performance begins with music. The director announces the scenes, but nothing actually appears. First, he announces Samson grasping the columns of the temple. Then he talks of a bull charging into the audience. Though the onlookers see nothing, they fling themselves on the ground in terror, insisting on protesting that they are true Christians and legitimate off-spring of their parents. The governor's daughter now feels the horns of the bull attacking her. The director's ideas keep increasing in boldness. He lets loose a swarm of mice into the audience. Only the mayor says he sees nothing happening, but later he too pretends to see them.

One may imagine how exciting are the theatrical effects produced by the invisible mice that allegedly crawl up under the women's garments. After the mice, holy water from Jordan is poured over the audience. Then come lions and bears. And at the end the beautiful Herodias comes on and invites the gentlemen to dance with her. When a man in the audience objects that for a Jewish princess she does not seem to be majestically enough garbed, the director retorts briefly that there is an exception to every rule. The mayor's nephew at last has the courage to dance a saraband with the invisible partner, a rich theatrical effect.

At that moment a quartermaster comes bursting in, demanding billets for thirty horsemen. The audience, thinking he is only another figure in this theater of wonders, do not take him seriously. But when they realize he does not see the lovely Herodias, they accuse him of being a new Christian and set upon him. During the general brawl, the director and his woman companion seize the curtain, which is their sole property, wrap it up, and disappear with the entrance fees, which they have prudently pocketed away at the start.

This short play, which is of frightening relevancy to us in our present day, demonstrates Cervantes's dramatic instinct.

Lope de Vega Carpio (1562–1635)

1562: Born in Madrid. His parents, Félix de Vega Carpio and Francisca Fernandez Florez, sewing craftsmen, had come to the capital nine months earlier from the Cantabrian north of Spain.

1567: Probably writes earliest poems.

1575: Lope becomes a page to the bishop of Cartagena and Avila. Writes his first comedia.

1578: Lope's father dies. Lope is a brilliant student at the Jesuit College and the Royal Academy in Madrid. It is reported that he ran away once, escaping to Segovia, where he was apprehended by the police. After completing his studies at the universities of Madrid and Alcalá, he entered into the theatrical profession.

1583: As a soldier under Don Álvaro de Bazán he fights against Portugal, which had been annexed to Spain in 1581, in the Azores. Subsequently he serves as secretary to the Marqués de las Navas, who allows him ample leisure to write.

1587: He is arrested in the Corral de la Cruz, at the Madrid theater, and charged with libeling the theater producer Jerónimo Velásquez, whose daughter he loves. Is banished from Madrid.

1588: Marries Isabel de Urbina against the wishes of her parents. Soon after, he enlists in the royal navy. Fights in the battle of the Armada against England on the admiral's ship *San Juan*. After wanderings and misadventures the ship goes up in flames outside Coruña. But Lope is not yet permitted to return to Madrid.

1589: Lope's mother dies. He moves to Valencia, where he soon becomes celebrated as a writer for the stage. Every two months messengers carry one of his plays to Madrid.

1593: He becomes secretary to Don Antonio de Alba, a grandson of the famous and notorious Duke of Alba. Now alternates his residence between Toledo and Alba de Tormes, near Salamanca.

1596: Returns to Madrid and becomes the secretary and friend of the Duke of Sessa.

1598: His wife Isabel dies. The same year he marries Juana de Guardo, daughter of a wealthy butcher. The poet Luis de Góngora jeers at this marriage of expediency. Don Pedro Fernandez de Castro, the promoter of Cervantes, becomes Lope's patron.

1599: Lope takes part as an actor in the splendid celebration of the double wedding of Philip III and his sister in Valencia.

1602: The actress Micaela de Luján, whom he calls Lucinda in his poems, becomes his mistress and the mother of seven of his children. One is his favorite daughter Marcela, a poetically gifted girl, who later enters a convent.

1604: The first collected edition of his works appears, according to which 203 of his plays have already been produced.

1611:   Lope enters a minor church order.

1613:   His second wife, Juana, dies. He becomes a priest after the death of his little son Carlos. His liaison with the poet Marta de Navares, whom he calls his Tenth Muse, becomes the talk of Madrid. She later loses her mind and dies in blindness. Lope remained true to her to the end. Marcelino Menéndez y Pelayo said: "He was a passionately religious believer and an unregenerate sinner all in one person."

1617:   Volumes 9 to 20 of the complete edition of his plays appear, with a foreword written by himself.

1627:   Pope Urban VIII confers the title of Doctor of Theology on him.

1628:   Lope becomes pastor of the Congregation of Saint Peter.

1635:   He dies unexpectedly 27 August after a brief illness. The Duke of Sessa provides an elaborate funeral for him. The whole country joins in mourning for him. Five bishops conduct obsequies for him during nine days, 150 eulogies are pronounced over him. Was buried in the Church of Saint Sebastian in Madrid.

Lope de Vega, the most prolific dramatist known in the western world, wrote in all fifteen hundred plays, of which four hundred seventy have been preserved; the titles of seven hundred seventy are known to us. In addition we have from his pen three full novels, four long stories, nine verse epics, three didactic poems, numerous occasional pieces, and about three thousand sonnets. He is said to have composed many of his plays within the span of twenty-four hours. Cervantes said of him that he was "one of nature's marvels," and "the reigning monarch of the stage." The customary expression in his day for anything good and praiseworthy in Spain was: "It's by Lope," and it sounded almost sacrilegious when his innumerable admirers would word their confession of faith by the formula: "I believe in Lope, the almighty poet of heaven and earth."

Cervantes, the most gifted writer of the period, was the first to recognize Lope de Vega, fifteen years his junior, as the preeminent genius among Spanish dramatists. By taking this stand he clearly differed from writers who revered the drama of antiquity, such as Pedro Simón Abril, the adapter of Terence and Aristophanes, or López de Villaboe, the translator of Plautus. These men had become the spokesmen for classical theater in Spain. But their efforts proved fruitless. The popular won out over the academic theater.

Three forms of Spanish drama coexisted in the last third of the sixteenth century. One was the heir of the drama of antiquity, which was not only influenced but initiated by the Italian Renaissance. This never achieved public acceptance. Another was the sensation-filled drama written by playwrights who imitated Seneca. This was considered outside of Spain as typically Spanish. The third was the folk play, in which religious and worldly motives were intermingled, and which reflected both the comic and the tragic. By the turn of the century the first two of these had gradually been overshadowed by the third. This direction was dictated little by innate demand or taste in the audiences. What actually brought it about was the circumstance that Lope de Vega, the most talented Spanish dramatist of his day, found that this form lent itself to his gifts, whereupon he proceeded to develop it into a vehicle of great art.

Lope de Vega is considered to be the founder of the Spanish theater. He stands at the core of Spain in a double sense: he was a man of the middle class, and he was born and brought up in Madrid. He was a writer of great eloquence, not a visionary writer. His plays were almost always written on commission. He was the servant of the theater.

It would be wrong to conclude from his unconventional private life that he did not strictly comply with the regulations of state and church. A minor functionary of the Inquisition, anything revolutionary or heretical was foreign to him. "In its underlying concepts his stage was not satirical; he was content with the existing condition and the prevailing views" (Vossler).

Lope de Vega made use of every sort of material that came to his hand. National sagas, heroic legends, contemporary literature of his own or other countries, even private or political happenings of the day—all served equally as his sources. To speak of Lope's theater is to speak of a living topical theater—a theater that had existed only once before in Europe, the theater of ancient Greece. But with all its brightness of treatment this topicality is never merely ephemeral gossip. It is always a screen to conceal a higher and timeless reality. "The basic characteristic of all his dramas is the unconcealed joy he takes in all the unexpected chances of life as the evidences, the disguises, and the disclosures of a reality that cannot be more immediately apprehended" (Vossler).

The purpose of comedy, as Lope unassumingly defined it, is "to copy the actions of mankind and depict the customs of the times." Yet it is, at most, a reflection, not a portrait, of reality. The Spanish theater had its own conception of reality. In terms of the representation of reality in contemporary theater it can probably be described, although only approximately, as what we call realism in contradistinction to naturalism.

Both the academic and the popular traditions inter-penetrate in Lope's work. He admired the classics but preferred the "barbarian joyous taste for marvels" of his own people. Significant of this attitude is his own expression in his manual of playwriting *The New Art of Writing Plays*: "When I have the task before me of writing a play, first I lock up all the rules under seven seals."

But however much Lope accommodated himself to the preferences of his audience, however accurate was the label—the house poet of the Madrid theater—given him, the poet in him dominated the script writer in most of his plays. Franz Grillparzer, who wrote exten-sively on Lope de Vega, considering him his most important master, characterized the poetic quality of Lope's work most aptly: "When a situation occurred to him that interested him as a poet, he would apply the whole of his incomparable talent to it. If the story were altogether of that nature, his entire treatment of it would be masterful." He also wrote: "While Lope never wrote a whole play that can be called superior throughout, it is also true that he never wrote a play in which there is not at least one scene that equals the best that Shakespeare ever wrote."

Lope dramatized everything that seemed suitable to him, asking only that the material be stimulating. When a subject seemed to him too copious for one comedia, or when it offered so many possibilities for variations, he divided it up into several plays. Some-times he handled his material in the manner of a serial story, in which he ended the play with a cliff-hanger in order to make the audience eager to see the next episode. His principal requirement was that the subject be Spanish or be capable of being hispanicized. This was one of the obvious concessions he had to make to his audience, which wanted to see itself in their theater. Although he realized that such a concession posed some danger to his artistry, he reconciled himself to it by explaining the true purpose of his comedias with this ironic expression of resignation: "We must please the people according to their own tastes even if art thereby goes out the window."

It was precisely this audience that unremittingly spurred him to write new works, this public that possessed an almost unbelievably genuine culture of its own. This audience welded public and dramatist into an inseparable, mutually interpenetrating and fructifying unity, witnessed to by the increasing excellence of the actors' performances. These actors, and especially their directors, contributed largely to Lope's work. He wrote for specific companies, for specific actors. This procedure markedly heightened the impact of his plays. In the years in which theater was prohibited, he wrote nothing. He had to have the direct contact with the living stage.

His idolization by the public that cheered his comedias unreservedly was in marked contrast to the reception given to those who were writing dramas according to literary rules. Luis de Góngora y Argote (1561–1627), slavishly following aesthetic maxims, was at the opposite pole artistically from Lope. It is significant that this unquestionably highly gifted lyric poet failed as a dramatist. His failure was due not so much, as has been asserted, to his lack of objectivity (a certain amount of which is essential for a dramatist) as to his inability to feel rapport with an audience that was made up not of a few aesthetes but of a great variety of different types of individuals.

It speaks well for Lope de Vega that his attacks on Góngorism were directed not so much at the person of Góngora himself, whom in fact he greatly respected, as against the numerous followers of Góngora, who preached the gospel of Góngorism as the only acceptable literary style. Lope, who experimented with all literary styles, attempted briefly—without success—to compose in the Góngora manner. He soon reverted to his own individual style. His audience not unexpectedly was an enthusiastic ally in scoffing at Góngorism.

Lope won his victory over the Góngorists not so much by his well-aimed shafts as by the responses of theatergoers to the impact of his plays.

New opponents continued to emerge. In 1617 he was charged by the learned scholar Cristóbal Suárez de Figueroa with currying favor with the masses. In the same year, in the magazine *Spongia* appearing in Paris, his person as well as his work were attacked and most shamefully abused. But in the following year a rejoinder, *Expostulatio Spongiae*, appeared. It was written by partisans of Lope, not the least of whom was the professor of Greek at the University of Alcalá. Lope was passionately defended in it. It asserted that Lope had the right to develop his own theory of art. The brochure pointed out that Lope had taken all nature for his pattern and was more conscious than most others of the changing views and mores of the time. "Lope has not only created a genuine art form but has surpassed the art of the ancients with his."

For all that, Lope himself never regarded his comedias as the highest fulfillment of his literary genius even though his deepest affection belonged to the theater. In his eyes his epic and lyric compositions were his most artistic works. This opinion was perhaps influenced by the circumstance that his dramatic writing served an immediate purpose; the play was an object to be brought to realization by actors. He was also affected by the rapidity with which production followed the writing, which made it impossible for him to polish a work or even to read it carefully. He was often obliged to give the actors what he had just written the previous day. Some of his comedias were written and produced within a span of two weeks.

In the introduction to volume fifteen of his comedias (1617) he apologized for the apparently superficial style of his work. He said: "This writer does what he can for his comedias, but because other commitments hinder him, he cannot revise the texts as carefully as he would like to. It would be impossible to publish them in the form in which they were first handed to the actors." That is, in preparing the plays for publication, he has incorporated revisions made in the course of production. But he added:

> The plays I present here are written in a language that would be considered old-fashioned by today's playwrights. It is also strange that many regard as valuable only what they cannot understand. . . . This writer does not wish to praise his own work or underrate that of younger playwrights. He surely has shown some ability in his other writings and so is content to leave these comedias as untended field-grown wildflowers in his *vega*. [Lope means rabbit; Vega means meadow.]

And it reads like a reply to criticism when, two hundred years later, in 1839, Grillparzer wrote of him:

> There never was another writer in the world in whom the highest poetic gift worked hand in hand with the most lighthearted carelessness as they

did in Lope. The writing of verses had become such a necessity to him and the demand for new plays so insistent that he threw his clay on the wheel and left it to mood and chance whether it would emerge as a vase or an ordinary pitcher.

Grillparzer also wrote:

> The further one reads in Lope's works, the more astounding are the riches of the talent we encounter, and in the end we must admit that, allowing for all his defects and his negligence, his equal can hardly be found in his fidelity to nature, his artistic sensibility, his infinite variety, and his gift of portraiture.

Lope enjoyed fame in his lifetime such as is rare among writers, but it was rather the glory of a man of the theater, the enthusiasm for a star of the stage, than the renown of a poet. Even then he belonged more to the theater than to literature. All Spain called him its phoenix. He was regarded as highly at the royal court as he was among the common people. He was celebrated equally as the man who wrote plays true to nature about everyday life as the writer of impressive religious dramas. He succeeded in fusing tales of court life and of lowly life. He raised to a higher level stories that had hitherto been routine cloak-and-sword exercises. He became the incarnation of the three elements so indigenous to Spain: nature, theater, and religion.

Lope's life was lived in extremes, a life of abandoning himself to passion and remorse, to licentiousness and mortification of the flesh. But he succeeded in fusing these opposites within himself into a unified man. It was he who incited to a still higher degree the Spaniard's passion for the theater. In a matter of very few years its repertory contained more than ten thousand plays. In another hundred years this number was even doubled. Playwriting became the fashion. It became a mania. Quantity, understandably, outran quality. As early as 1608 we learn from a passage in one of Francisco Quevedo y Villegas's novels how widespread the rage for playwriting had become:

> We were giving a play based on a picaresque novel, *Vida del buscón*, that one of our company had written. I was surprised that any actor could write plays. I had thought that only very erudite and wise men could compose, not ordinary laymen like us. But things have reached the stage where there are no longer any theater directors who do not write comedias themselves, and no longer any actors who have not delivered themselves of a Moorish or Christian farce. I can remember when it was different and we hardly had anything else in the way of comedias than those by the most excellent Lope de Vega or by Alonso Ramón.

In 1617 Suárez de Figueroa inveighed against the concessions dramatists were making to "the plebeian point of view of the masses." It is likely that most dramatists were themselves men of the people. The anecdote about the illiterate tailor in Toledo who engaged a scribe so he could publish the plays he composed may be very telling in its irony.

Today it would be difficult to establish the extent of intentional plagiarism in the common practice of presenting as new works the adaptations of plays already well known. We must, however, not characterize this practice in twentieth-century terms. Even the greatest writers like Lope de Vega and Calderón used plays already available as source material for their own. At

times the demand for material to slake the voracious
thirst for new dramas was so urgent that several writers
would collaborate to write a play to order.

The literary critics misjudged the situation. For these
remote spirits the living theater in the *corrales* was
only a means for satisfying primitive appetites for low-
class entertainment. For them only true poetry could
be classified as dramatic art. Once again in theater
history the confusion between literary and dramatic
principles conjured up the danger of splitting theater
into one for the people and one for the educated
classes confounding literary with theatrical principles.
(About a hundred years later in Germany, the literary
theoretician Johann Christoph Gottsched, 1700–1766,
did succeed in vanquishing the theater people.) But
during Spain's golden age the primacy of the popular
theater prevailed. This was not so much because of the
passion for the theater of a monarch such as Philip IV
as because of the fact that this popular Spanish theater
had the good fortune to attract a series of such inspired
poets as Lope de Vega, Tirso de Molina, Juan Ruiz
de Alarcón, and Calderón.

In Spain itself the comedias of the golden age faded
off the boards around the turn of the seventeenth
century, a phenomenon I have discussed earlier. It took
a longer perspective, a more historical approach to
these works, together with the awakening of a new
Spanish nationalism after Napoleon's military occupa-
tion, to lead Spain to a rediscovery of the great
comedia writers.

Lope de Vega's direct and indirect influence on the
theater was even stronger than on literature in general.
I cannot conceive of any of the baroque forms of
theater that were predominant in the eighteenth

century, either the great spiritual works of the religious orders, or the festival theater of the courts, or the temporary stages of the wandering comedians, as having existed had there been no Lope.

Lope de Vega's mythological festival play *The Golden Fleece* was presented in Spanish at the Vienna Court Theater in 1633. (Other comedias were also played in Spanish there.) The first ascertainable production of a comedia by Lope in German took place in Zittau in 1661, when *The Palace Disordered* was presented. According to some authorities, this play was earlier presented in Hamburg in 1652. Since the middle of the seventeenth century the announcements of the repertories of German touring companies include numerous comedias by Lope. It seems unlikely that these were played by Spanish actors. It is more probable that they were offered by traveling troupes that regularly played in Italy, France, the Netherlands, or Belgium. It cannot be doubted that these, like the drastically altered versions of Shakespeare being produced in that period, were offered as comedias in which the gracioso, transformed into a buffoon, became the principal character of the play.

The shunting aside of true emotion and the substitution of the witty gracioso by a coarse jester brought the Spanish comedia into discredit with such observers as, for instance, the Danish writer Ludvig Holberg. Thus it is not surprising that during the age of Gottsched's classicism, the last remnants of the Spanish comedia disappeared from the stage.

The famous revival of the theater during the German romantic movement hardly skimmed the surface of Lope's achievement. With some justice, Spain was called the Hellas of the romanticists, but Lope de Vega was of only limited consequences in this Hellas. "His

comedias," wrote August Wilhelm Schlegel, the
famous translator of Shakespeare, "are like clusters that
a witty writer of skits chalks up on paper without any
previous preparation, without taking time to think on
which every unconsidered stroke of his hasty careless-
ness has life and meaning. Apart from lacking careful
and conscientious structure, Lope's work is lacking in
depth and in those finer relationships that, after all,
constitute the mysterious in art."

In the opinion of the romanticists Lope's most serious
failing is that artistic instinct that makes human
intellect go nature one better, the quality that seems
so estimable in Calderón. Obviously it was not worth-
while even to try to present any of Lope's comedias.
Even Grillparzer's sympathetic intercession for Lope,
and his emphasis on Lope's being true to nature—
which, it is true, contained an intentional defiance of
the German romanticists and their enthusiasm for
Calderón's mannerisms—was not enough to effect the
admission of Lope to the stage.

It was not until the twentieth century that Lope de
Vega penetrated the theater outside Spain. Today, in
France and Germany, his comedias are performed fre-
quently by repertory theaters.

In America, Lope continues to live in the university
theater. One of his most popular plays today, both in
Spain and in the United States, is *Fuente Ovejuna*
(literally, "watering place of sheep"), the name of a
village in Andalusia. The plot deals with a historical
incident in 1476 in which the meek people of Fuente
Ovejuna, after suffering extreme indignities at the
hands of a local overlord, overthrew and killed the
ruthless tyrant. The straw that evoked this deed was
the abduction of Laurencia, the mayor's daughter, on
her wedding day. When he questioned anyone in the

town, the king's investigating magistrate met only with the answer "Fuente Ovejuna lo hizo" ("Fuente Ovejuna killed him"), a saying that still exists in Spain today as a response to unwelcome questions. Faced with punishing the entire village, King Ferdinand instead pardoned everyone.

In 1966 the theater department of Northwestern University in Evanston, Illinois, presented an outstanding production of this favorite under the title *The Sheep-Well*. Lee Mitchell, the director, in an article for the *Drama Critique* (spring 1966), reviewed some of the problems of producing a seventeenth-century Spanish play for a modern-day American audience.

As Mr. Mitchell saw it, the "pronounced musico-romantic nature of the play" held the best potential for audience appeal. To achieve this quality, he cast the performance with versatile actors who could perform the reasonably easy folk dances of seventeenth-century Spain, chosen by Carmen Mayoral, the dance director, and sing the many lyrics Lope incorporated. In his description of this charming production Mr. Mitchell wrote:

> The victorious Commander was welcomed by the peasants with a *Bal de Cercolets*, a lovely serpentine with flower arches forming an arbor for the entrance of the Commander and his troops. The wedding of Laurencia and Frondoso was celebrated with an *Ave Maria*, a round dance for twelve, after which the bride and bridegroom took the stage for a spirited *Ole de la Curra* with castanets. As these two were our most gifted dancers, this number always brought down the house. For the exaltation after the revolt we used a *Seguidilla*, a simple staccato square dance for sixteen with heel beats. For the finale all the

peasants joined in a joyous dance, *A lo Alto y a lo Bajo*, terminating in a duet by Laurencia and Frondoso.

To carry out his musical-comedy interpretation, Mr. Mitchell used seventeenth-century costuming rather than the dress of 1476 primarily because it was richer and handsomer, and the audience was offered a feast of colorful folk dress, silk capes, plumed helmets, and rich brocades.

In February 1970 the Theater Arts Division of Columbia University made its debut with a presentation of *Fuente Ovejuna*. George Gent, of the *New York Times* (13 February 1970), wrote that "its traditional form and contemporary ambience are precisely right for the young players."

Dr. Bernard Beckerman, chairman of the Theater Arts Division and director of the play, explained that this long, heroic work, which made great demands on the young performers, was chosen because: " 'Fuente Ovejuna' is a classic play with contemporary relevance in that it was one of the first to depict a community of workers and peasants as capable of courage and resolution."

Another Lope de Vega play that is frequently performed in the United States is his *Gardener's Dog*. Here Lope skillfully applied the psychology of the Aesopian fable of the dog in the manger to a charming story in the human realm. Doña Diana's maid is in love with Diana's secretary, Teodoro. When Diana learns of this, she herself falls in love with Teodoro. Although she will not confess her love to him because he is of a lower social position than she, she will not allow her maid to have him either. And when Teodoro admits to Diana that he loves her, she arrogantly puts him in his place. Lope demonstrates a subtle sense of the psychology of women as he skillfully shows Diana's vacillation between pride and bewilderment, arrogance and love. As always, love wins out in the end—but only after Teodoro's servant reveals to Diana that Teodoro is the long lost son of the nobleman Don Ludovico (a story he has invented to further his master's interests).

One interesting production of *The Gardener's Dog* was that of the Yiddish Art Theater in New York in 1927, which used an adaptation written and directed by Boris Glagolin. A more recent production is that of the Little Theater School of Fine Arts at Texas Christian University in 1963. Under the title of *The Dog in the Manger*, this production used the prose translation of Jill Booty, whose translations of Lope are acknowledged to be the best in English.

Georges Neveux's excellent translation of *The Gardener's Dog* (*Le chien du jardinier*, 1955) has become a favorite item of repertory theater. His version had its premiere in a production at the Théâtre Marigny in Paris, in which Jean-Louis Barrault played Teodoro and Madeleine Renaud played Doña Diana. Barrault also directed the play.

It is not easy to discern why Lope has won such a place in our time. The steadily increasing importance, since the turn of the century, of the function of the stage director, is surely not the least of the factors that has contributed substantially to this result. The stage director seeks above all a good script. It is not the written word but the comic potentialities inherent in a play that interests him.

The lack of real comedies these days in the German repertory, especially now that the comedy of social situation is no longer popular, is another factor that may have furthered the rediscovery of the old comedias. The cloak-and-sword comedia is more manageable than the *comedia dell'arte* plays, which are almost unplayable by non-Italian actors, and offers much richer variety. And the audiences respond to it with evident joy. This makes the comedias of Lope de Vega and his contemporaries indispensable elements of the current repertory, giving ensemble actors a respite between the serious classics and the severe moderns.

Only a *fait accompli* will tell us if a Lope de Vega comedia can succeed in being relevant to our times. Lope de Vega, a theater man to his very marrow, himself would be the last to protest against free interpretation and the necessary adaptation of his works if theatrical success were to be obtained by such treatment.

To illustrate the genius of Lope I have chosen three theatrical masterpieces: *Not So Stupid After All*, *Sir Miracle Comes a Cropper*, and *The Madmen of Valencia*.

Not So Stupid After All

Lope de Vega wrote this farce for the actress Jeronima de Burgos in 1613, when he was secretary to the Duke of Sessa. A true cloak-and-sword comedia in its structure, a piece of entertainment suitable for any audience, it is a striking satire on the times. Even more it is a variant of the basic theme of all Spanish drama—that life is only an illusion.

Don Liseo is en route to Madrid to meet his fiancee, a daughter of the rich Don Octavio. He and his manservant, who is interested only in what he can get to eat, meet a student who tells them that Don Octavio in fact has two daughters. They are both as pretty as pictures, but while one is intelligent and interested in knowledge, the other is so hopelessly stupid that she will receive a dowry unequalled in Madrid.

It is the stupid one, Doña Finea, who is betrothed to Liseo. This news makes him very unhappy. While the intelligent sister, Doña Nise, carries on intellectual conversations, the stupid Finea resists any effort by her tutor to teach her to read. Lope de Vega makes use of Nise's appearances to poke fun at the elaborate lyrics of the Góngorists, which must have aroused much merriment in his audience. He has Nise say that poetry sometimes soars to such elevated heights that it is almost inaudible. One can only feel it: "And it is wrapped in a thousand veils that decorate it so that the words that strike our ears are only dim and dark." To this her cook Celia remarks: "Dark! Obscure because nobody can understand them. That's why so many chatter about them so learnedly." Nise's reply to this is no less indicative: "What more do you want, Celia?" she says, "Everything in the world is only sham and deception. We won't change that."

After the scene that introduces both maidens as they have been described, three cavaliers turn up to pay court to Doña Nise. They are students, all three of them. On one level, this play is a satire on the snobbism of the intelligentsia. Accordingly, it is a sonnet, correctly crafted according to academic rules, which the leading suitor tries to enchant Doña Nise with. We gather the derision Lope was expressing from the opinion on this sonnet expressed by another suitor: "Who would be so bold as to criticize your sonnet if he is not bold enough to understand it?"

Doña Nise herself is portrayed as being very susceptible to intellectual delights, but in a way that makes it obvious nobody in the audience will take her interest seriously. A "learned lady" was a type in fashion at the time, a type we shall encounter again in Moreto's Doña Diana. Don Laurencio, one of the competitors for Doña Nise's hand, has this to say about such "learned ladies":

"It is never satisfactory if women are too clever
In marriage, for a woman's strength
Ought not to lie in knife-edged thinking.
That, Pedro, is the sickness of our times,
The women getting smarter every day.
They do indeed almost behave like men,
They're selfish, calculating, inconsiderate,
Not warm, not cool. Neither fish are they
    nor are they fowl."

The gracioso Pedro says it much more simply: "Learned ladies are just not bearable."

After reciting his sonnet, the poetical suitor begins to discourse on various kinds of heat, from that of the blazing sun to that of the fire of love. This is becoming too much even for the clever Nise. Don Laurencio now begins to take alarm at Nise's cleverness, and he tries, surely not least on account of Finea's rich dowry, to turn his attention toward Finea, the stupid sister. As if conjured up, Finea is just passing by, and a highly amusing garden scene takes place.

First, Laurencio and Finea cross the stage, talking about love. Then his manservant does the same with Finea's maid. Each couple talks his own style, but the gambits of the one are reflected by the other as in a mirror. Then the necessary entanglements begin to evolve. Nise falls in love with Laurencio, who has turned to Finea who is beginning to respond to his wooing. But she is loved by Liseo, who is affianced to Finea. This leads the two suitors to the point of a duel because Liseo assumes that Laurencio is his rival for Nise's love. This misunderstanding is fortunately cleared up in time. They become friends.

Now, however, love, in the droll way it has, had gradually been awakened in Finea. Arousing latent qualities in her, she becomes much shrewder. Right-thinking like all fathers in Spanish comedias are, though of limited awareness, her father is very pleased to see this. His other daughter's intellectual pretensions cause·him much more worry. Upon the advice of an old friend of his, Nise is to be married to the sonnet-writing suitor, Duardo.

This situation gives Lope de Vega another opportunity to poke fun at the fashionable aesthetes: "A man who can't do anything but write sonnets," says the father to his girls, "is more than unwelcome to me for a son-in-law!" From the conventional social point of view, the comment of Don Miseno is very interesting. He is trying to endorse the suit of his young friend. He says to the father: "You are mistaken. Duardo is a gentleman. He does not write poetry for a living."

Liseo now realizes that he is not the object of Nise's love. As Finea seems to have become smarter he begins to try to get closer to Finea, to whom he is engaged. But Finea has become more than merely clever. To rid herself of the suitor she does not herself love, she pretends to be as stupid as she was at the start. She manages to hide Laurencio, whom her father wanted to turn out of his home. Meanwhile, Nise's love has been awakened for Liseo (no doubt mainly to serve

the purposes of the play). After the general disen-
tanglement in the closing scene, the father gives both
pairs his blessing. Finea, supposed to be the stupid one,
has outmaneuvered her clever sister. She has got
Laurencio, the man Nise originally wanted. Duardo,
the poetry-writing cavalier, has made his effort in vain.
Love has won out over stupidity. To quote an observation of the two graciosos: "Only the stupid are clever
in this house, and all clever people are fools when they
are in love."

Not So Stupid After All is among the very best of
the cloak-and-sword comedias. The ingredients—the
complications, the love scenes in the garden, the challenge to a duel, the mirror play by the servants—have
never been done better.

This comedia rapidly conquered the German stage.
It was produced in the 1956–1957 season in the Berlin
Schloßparktheater.

The critics were unanimous in approving the performance of the actors in this production. The meta-
morphosis of Doña Finea, from the stupid girl who
showed almost pathological limitations, to the affectionate woman in love, was beautifully done. The way
"she blossomed out under the miracle of her great love
from her previous utter lack of awareness was a little
masterpiece of the art of acting," wrote one critic
about Käthe Braun's performance.

There was more controversy over the settings by
Dietrich Haugk. The "supermodern" settings were
objected to by some as being unsuited to Lope. It was
called a stylization that "unexpectedly pressed all the
juice out of the Spanish hothouse plant." Just this kind
of stylization was seen by others as exactly suited to
Lope as it required only a minimum of stage properties.

Sir Miracle Comes a Cropper

It is strange that this comedia, justly called equal to any one of Shakespeare's comedies, was rediscovered as suitable for the stage only in the mid-1900s. Even Grillparzer passed over this one in his discussion of the individual plays of Lope de Vega. Its ironic treatment of the Spanish cavalier must have elicited an unusual effect on the audience of the time.

The earliest printed version is found in Lope's collected plays (volume fifteen), which appeared in 1617. In that edition this comedia carries the subtitle *The Arrogant Spaniard*. This criticism of his own people has been interpreted as recognition of the political and social decline of the Spanish nation. In the baroque era the cavalier is no longer seen in the traditional way—the exemplar of loyalty, generosity, hospitality, protector of the weak, courageous knight. Instead every one of such qualities is closely scrutinized. The heir of the Reconquista goes to his defeat as the gallant Don Juan or a hungry idler in a picaresque story.

The cavalier now only plays at being a cavalier; he is no longer really one. Appearance must substitute for reality. The form simulates a content that no longer exists. From another point of view, a common man now tries to act the cavalier, but he can only mimic the forms. He cannot really play the part without being of noble birth. The Spanish soldier, whom Lope so successfully made the protagonist of many farces, out of his own recollections, now appears as only the descendant of the *miles gloriosus*. Now that Spain is in a period of decline when nobody takes the power of Spain seriously any longer, real Spanish pride is turned into mere external appearance, into empty arrogance. This fact is contrasted to the respect accorded to a Spaniard at the time of the rise of his country to world leadership and to enormous political success and influence.

The picaro type best known in the stories, the cavalier sunk to the level of a pseudocavalier as well as the proletarian risen to the level of a pseudocavalier, became a favorite character of the stage. I do not, however, believe that Lope de Vega set out to portray this relationship between political decline and the spurious affectation of cavalier status in this play.

To him the "arrogant" Spaniard was only a disagreeable type who merited scorn. In addition, the play is set a hundred years before Lope lived, in the reign of Charles V, that is, in the days when Spain was at the height of its power. Lope's scorn is directed not against an institution but against excesses of society. Vossler hit the mark more accurately when he characterized this play as "an airy persiflage on Spanish boastfulness and swaggering."

The scene corresponds to the structure of the stage of the time. It is a genuine cloak-and-sword comedia scene: a street, a small square in the background, the entrance to an inn, houses with balconies.

The action of the play is laid in Rome. Lope did not choose that setting because of the political or the ecclesiastical importance of the city. He probably set the play in Rome because it was the city of international pleasure-seekers in which impostors from the whole world meet women companions, who, though outwardly elegant, in fact practice a well-recognized profession. Luzmán, the protagonist, is a Spanish ex-officer in reduced circumstances who would like to be a cavalier. To his intense regret, he can lay claim to only peasant ancestry.

In an introductory conversation with his gracioso, Tristán, he describes himself accurately: what counts in life is to keep up appearances. It is not important to be what one really is. Fashionable clothing for men, cosmetics for women, cover up one's deficiencies. Even love must be dissembled, as its only purpose is to fortify one's self-confidence. At bottom, Luzmán really despises all women; an officer cannot do otherwise.

It is worthy of comment that Tristán, who is prepared to further any trick his master may devise, inwardly condemns this attitude. He rejects it not on moralistic grounds, but because he has reached a very natural and logical conclusion that one-sided love brings no joy even to the ardent one: "Just remember, if only yourself you love and no feeling have for women, if you have no love to give, you will get no joy from women." Tristán is the gracioso with a sound understanding of people. He is less the blatantly comic figure than the adviser and accomplice. He is true to his position as the servant but only so long as he can count on his master's gratitude.

More controlling than Luzmán's vanity is his eagerness for gain and honors. His adventures are the opposite of Don Quixote's. Don Quixote is inspired by the heightened idealism of Spanish chivalry, but Luzmán's adventures must pay off in money. Otherwise the risks he takes make no sense.

Luzmán's paramour, the Spanish courtesan Octavia, comes to him in despair to complain of Leonato's unbridled desire for her. Luzmán pledges himself to shed blood to protect her honor. This makes her fear for his life, and she seeks to restrain his rashness. But she has hardly left the room when he tells Tristán that he was only putting on an act. He has not the faintest intention of getting himself into a fight for her. Leonato, on the other hand, who is in a rage because he blames Luzmán for Octavia's rejection of him, wants to challenge Luzmán to a duel.

Leonato's servant, Camillo, a second gracioso, a somewhat more humorous figure than Tristán, tries fruitlessly to restrain Leonato. Camillo is above all a judge of women par excellence. Luzmán has the reputation of being a fearless knight. The Spanish audience is likely to have caught on quickly to the mockery with which the following speech is imbued: "Luzmán comes, as you do, from the coast of Spain. How ardently he burns with honor. Even the most cowardly wretch who comes from there is wholly captivated by his own sense of worth."

When at last the two "heroes" meet, the situation has altered completely. Leonato does not recognize Luzmán, but Luzmán knows very well who Leonato is. Luzmán asks Leonato to exchange cloaks with him to help him elude pursuit. As such courtesies were assumed and taken for granted among cavaliers, Leonato agrees. But Luzmán's only object in this ruse is to come to Octavia in Leonato's garments and boast of having won them in a duel.

Meanwhile the go-between Lofraso has drawn Luzmán's eye to a young Venetian woman, Isabela, who has arrived in Rome with a wealthy old husband. Now Luzmán is no longer interested in Octavia; his intentions are all focused on Isabela.

At this juncture a Walloon officer, his gracioso Lombardo, and his French paramour Beatriz arrive on the stage. The Walloon officer is the prototype of the courtly lover who tries to shine for his paramour by his superior cultivation. Lombardo is his opposite in every sense; he is a worldly contrast to the idealistic humbug that his master is.

Luzmán at once decides to benefit by the situation. He has the go-between, Lofraso, using the pretext of finding accommodations for the gentlemen, take Lombardo with him. Then Luzmán's servant, Tristán, is to challenge the Walloon to fight. The point is to have Beatriz left behind alone. The scheme works. Now Luzmán approaches her without interference, promises her the blue skies, and goes off with her.

When the Walloon, who has been trying futilely to catch up with the elusive Tristán, returns, he is told that Leonato has absconded with Beatriz. The result is a senseless free-for-all row between Leonato, who enters without knowledge of this accusation, the Walloon, and their respective servants. The first act closes on this fight, in which the fate of the three lovers—Luzmán, Leonato, and the Walloon—and three plots seem to be inextricably interwoven.

Now Luzmán gives Beatriz a gown and chain that Octavia had given him. He was supposed to turn it into money for his flight from a supposedly dangerous opponent.

He has not, however, given up his hope of winning Isabela, the beautiful Venetian. Now the audience is offered a common motif in the cloak-and-sword comedias. Isabela appears, heavily veiled, on her balcony. Luzmán carries on a conversation with two of his servants that he has carefully planned. They question Isabela's beauty. He defends it, even going so far as to threaten them with his sword to save the honor of his adored one. Isabela overhears this conversation, falls in love with Luzmán, and invites him in to her house.

Meanwhile Octavia has found out that Luzmán gave away her gown and chain to another woman. With the help of a new lover she attacks the unsuspecting Beatriz. Beatriz, in a scene that was hugely enjoyed by Spaniards, is disrobed in this attack down to her chemise. Isabela's elderly husband catches sight of her in this condition and instantly falls in love with her. He asks her in to his house. This leads to a fresh complication. Beatriz and Luzmán meet each other there, but with his smooth talk he gets himself out of this tight spot.

In the closing scene of this act the two servants admire their master's talent for artfully shining everywhere though he has nothing in his pocket. The second servant answers Tristán's skeptical praise with a formula reply: "It is for this that he is called Sir Miracle."

Luzmán now reenters, filled with new self-confidence. No longer does he want to believe he is of peasant ancestry. He prefers to claim descent from a count outside wedlock. On his servant's suggestion, he decides to call himself Don Luzmán of Toledo and Mendoza Giron Enriquez Lara. In a monologue Luzmán praises the advantages of noble descent. Nevertheless, he offers the conclusion that all earthly advancement is only illusion. The higher tribunal is no respecter of social classes. Lope de Vega probably expressed in this monologue his own sense of bitterness over the inequities of birth. But it says something significant about him and his times that this made him write a gay comedy, not a tragedy. After this moment of introspection Lope captivates his audience again by the motley medley of the adventures.

Now Leonato again encounters Luzmán. He is ready

to avenge the lie that attributed to him the conquest of Beatriz, who was wholly unknown to him. Again Luzmán succeeds in avoiding a fight. He manages to win Leonato's favor by flattering him with compliments, something no Spanish officer can resist. And he promises Leonato's servant, Camillo, beautiful women to compensate him for the insult. Finally Luzmán invites them both into the tavern but vanishes in time to avoid paying the bill.

Now, as a newly hatched nobleman, Luzmán decides to find new quarters and a new servant for himself, at Isabela's expense. Meanwhile the Walloon officer, who is still looking for Beatriz, finds Tristán (Luzmán's servant). He learns from Tristán the daringly mendacious news that Luzmán has lost Beatriz to a rich Venetian, who has shut her up in a house of joy to make money out of her. The Walloon officer, in a rage, creates a scene in front of Isabela's house, demanding the release of his paramour. Charged with being a noisy drunk, he is arrested and treated roughly. Luzmán succeeds in having the Walloon officer held by the police as allegedly insane. Once more Luzmán emerges as the hero of the episode.

The third act opens with a delightful love scene between Luzmán and Isabela. Each pretends mistrust by the same gestures, only to be able to celebrate an ecstatic reconciliation. Isabela promises Luzmán a substantial sum of gold. Luzmán has achieved his purpose. But again he runs into Leonato, who is now even more enraged at him. He now wants to get even for the tavern bill Luzmán dodged. This time Luzmán appeases him with a sonnet he composes to him. This at once compensates Leonato, who as a Spaniard is susceptible to poetry, for all the wrongs he had suffered at

Luzmán's hands. Here again Lope is taking potshots at the fashion of writing flattering poetry to Spanish gentlemen.

Meanwhile the Walloon officer has got himself released from the asylum. With his own servant he comes upon Tristán just as Tristán is getting Isabela's chest of gold for Luzmán. The officer and his man steal the chest. Tristán then has the brilliant idea of restoring Beatriz to the Walloon officer. In return Tristán is allowed to hold on to the money.

Now everything looks as if Luzmán has won out after all. As a rich man he can leave Rome and return to Spain. But when he tries to pay off Tristán with a ridiculously small amount, he digs his own grave. For this loyal servant, who has committed every sort of rascality for his master, and helped him out of many a scrape, is shocked at this monstrous ingratitude. He complains of his fate in front of Isabela's house. Overhearing his laments (and this is another theatrical devise) she learns the whole truth about Luzmán. In a rage, she advises Tristán to get companions and attack Luzmán. Tristán gets Leonato and Leonato's servant to help. Together they fall upon Luzmán, who is so sure of his victory and is about to depart on his journey.

Luzmán is robbed of everything. He is even deprived (in a parody parallel to the attack on Beatriz) of his clothing from his undershirt out. In despair Luzmán calls out to Isabela for help, but she sarcastically throws him a length of rope. Then he pleads to Beatriz for help, but she only laughs at him. Then he appeals to Octavia, who now having acquired a second gallant, only empties a bucket of water over his head. It is highly amusing to see how these appeals for help proceed on the stage. Luzmán rushes from window to window, but he now gets only derision and ridicule. His last hope is that help can be found in his own quarters, but Tristán has nothing but scorn left for him. The wet, semidressed Luzmán decides to go into a hospital.

One may see in this play not only a satire on the real Spanish cavalier but also a realistic presentation of the fashionable would-be cavalier. But I believe Lope was interested in mere entertainment, in caricature for its own sake, far more than in satire, in criticism, or in instruction. An interpreter of the play in our day may find in it various possibilities of contemporary interpretation, but a too consciously sociological or moralistic approach would impair the airy humor of the play.

Sir Miracle Comes a Cropper is said to have been premiered in 1619 in Saragossa.

In modern-day Germany it is often played in Hans Schlegel's translation. In his version, Schlegel took into consideration the difference between the German and the Mediterranean styles of acting. The Mediterranean actor needs many gestures for his style of expression and communication. It not only supplements speech; it actually brings it to full realization. The spectator understands the speech without explanation because of the movements not only of the hands but of the face and of the whole body. For the northern actor, speech itself is the only medium of communication. He shuns excessive gesture.

Therefore, when Lope provides a long monologue or a static dialogue, as he did at the very opening of *Sir Miracle Comes a Cropper*, these are effective in Mediterranean countries because of the gestures that naturally accompanied the speeches. For the northern actor, however, it is necessary to provide supplementary dialogue in the translation.

The production offered at the Akademietheater of Vienna in the 1952–1953 season was described as "sheer unadulterated entertainment." The curtain arose on a stylized street scene, in which the houses and even the horizon reflected a golden glow that maintained the joyous unreal atmosphere of the setting. The costumes also struck the same note of vibrant color. The tempo, as guided by the director Ulrich Bettac, carried one along without stumbling over all the implausibility of the plot. The pace did not allow the theatergoer to think things over. The irony of the direction, as well as the charm of the setting, won praise, but doubts arose over this very charm. Some critics complained that it created "too mild an ambiance" for the play, too civilized a production. In addition to the critics who saw the play as sheer entertainment, there were a few who interpreted the production as expressing social criticism.

It was a delightful stroke of stage direction to have Luzmán at the conclusion wafted away over the rooftops of Rome.

The Madmen of Valencia

The action takes place in the famous asylum in Valencia. The same asylum is the scene of many chapters in Lope's novel of adventure, *Pilgrim in His Own Land*. Lope must have known of this institution during the many years he lived in Valencia. It is also a matter of verifiable history that on the occasion of great religious festivals, like that of the Holy Innocents, the hospital was open to visitors so the inmates could beg alms of them.

Although it was not likely Lope's intention to exhibit in the theater the actual living conditions in the asylum, the sociological background is not without interest for us. The mental institution in Valencia was unlike the insane asylums of its time. Its primary difference lay in the fact that it was conducted like a hospital, not like a kind of prison. Adequate medical care and unhampered activity of the lesser afflicted were taken for granted. Bonds were applied only in serious cases. We hear nothing in this play about the mentally sick being possessed by devils or being identified with witches, an attitude that made such an affliction even more burdensome in the Middle Ages. In this comedia insanity is considered a psychological phenomenon and treated accordingly.

But the institution is presented only as a theatrically effective background for an ingenious comedia about the irrationality of love. As Lope did in several of his plays, he wrote himself into this one under the stage name of Belardo, a former poet, a madman among madmen. It may be that Lope himself acted the part of Belardo. The remarks his Belardo makes in *The Madmen of Valencia* must have been very amusing to his contemporary audience. The very idea of hearing the dramatist speak as an asylum inmate must have been fascinating. Among other things, he explains that poetry must not only have charm but must also be profitable. He complains that there are only nine muses but more than nine thousand poets.

The play opens with a meeting of two young noblemen who are friends, Floriano and Valerio. Floriano confesses that he has just killed Reinero in a duel over a lovely woman and is now a fugitive from justice.

What makes his situation so fraught with peril is that Reinero was a prince, the heir to the throne, and Floriano is only a nobleman. Valerio is unable to offer his friend any advice other than that he pretend to be insane and get himself admitted to the asylum, where he will be safest from pursuit by the police. Floriano agrees with this suggestion. Valerio goes to the asylum to make arrangements for admitting Floriano under the alias of Beltran.

Erifila, daughter of a distinguished family, arrives in Valencia in flight. She has eloped with her servant Leonato. Leonato is afraid they are being pursued by Erifila's relatives and pretends that he doubts her love. He finally robs her of her jewels and her garments. Left alone, she bemoans her suffering and to save the honor of her class, she admits to the audience she never really loved her servant. Apparently such rhetoric contributed more to developing the virtuous character of a noble lady than a confession of true love for one inferior in rank would have. At this point the scantily clad Erifila is found by two quite harmless idiots. As her story is not believed, she is assumed to be demented, and it is decided to take her to the asylum.

While this is happening, Laida, the maid of Fedra, niece of the director of the hospital, falls in love with the putative madman Floriano. When she confesses this to her mistress, Fedra asks: "Have you fallen in love with a madman?" Laida's answer is the key to the whole comedia. "Love is a kind of madness, and if it isn't, it's not love." When Fedra catches sight of Floriano, she too is stricken with the mania of love.

At this point Erifila, in restraints, is being brought into the hospital. Getting just a glimpse of her, Floriano falls in love with Erifila, and Erifila with Floriano.

Neither dares to admit it to the other. In a delightful scene, conducted entirely in asides, each declares his love to the audience. But alas and alack, the beloved of each is mentally deranged. Eventually they speak openly to each other. Though each believes he must continue to pretend he is mad, they confess their mutual love under the rose. But Valerio, who had seen Erifila earlier, had also fallen passionately in love at first sight.

After the director has put some clothes on Erifila and led her away, Floriano is visited by Valerio. Valerio confesses to his friend that he is in love with a beautiful madwoman.

The first act ends in this welter of love.

The borderline between normality and insanity seems to be dissolved. Floriano feels he will actually lose his mind if he has to lose his beloved madwoman. When Erifila sees Floriano talking to Fedra, she is consumed with jealousy. In the second scene, she and Floriano realize that neither one is truly insane. They confide their plights to each other. But when the director sees them together he has them put in restraints because it is a rule of the hospital that men and women patients must not fraternize.

Liberto now enters. He brings with him a picture of Floriano, who is being sought all through the country as the murderer of the prince Reinero. Learning of this, Floriano darkens his face with lampblack as a precaution against being recognized. A new love scene between him and Erifila is interrupted by the maid Laida. In her despair at finding she has a rival, she can think of nothing better than to pretend she is mad so as to be able to stay close to Floriano. Her mistress Fedra sees through her stratagem, and for the same reason, she too pretends to be mad. Now the free admission of love, which is forbidden in the world of the normal, is permitted among the mad.

Under the advice of the doctor, there is only one cure possible for Fedra. That is marriage to Floriano. Naturally this can only be a pretended ceremony. Floriano agrees to the doctor's prescription, which turns Erifila into his enemy. In bitterness she agrees to Valerio's plan. He will pretend to be a relative so he can get her released from the asylum. In spite of this Floriano is confident she will return to him.

Because it is the Feast of the Holy Innocents, guests are being awaited in the courtyard of the insane asylum. The audience is offered various kinds of insane people, who are ready to ask for alms. Belardo, Lope's alter ego, is among them.

A stranger, a wealthy nobleman, accompanied by Leonato the servant, arrives. (Leonato is the servant who so perfidiously robbed Erifila.) The stranger is shown the facilities of the asylum and is also invited to the wedding ceremony being arranged for Fedra and Floriano. Benches are set up for the guests and one waits for the nuptial ceremony. Leonato and Laida are to be the witnesses. Floriano, festively arrayed as a bridegroom, makes his entrance. But even before the ceremony begins he has an open quarrel with Fedra. This dialogue is interrupted by a wedding dance by the insane inmates, who make deep bows to the bridal couple in strange but highly theatrical gestures.

Now Erifila, followed by Valerio, bursts on the stage. In revenge, she intends to betray Floriano's secret—that he is the assassin who is being sought. Now the plot bids fair to become a tragedy. But the plot twists just in time. The noble stranger announces that he is really the prince Reinero, whom Floriano thought he killed. It was the prince's page, wearing the prince's colors, whom Floriano killed. This leaves Floriano innocent in the eyes of the law and the authorities.

Still to be settled is a contest between Floriano and his friend Valerio over the possession of Erifila, but the "happy ending" is inevitable. Floriano marries Erifila. Fedra marries Valerio. Laida marries Leonato, who has begged Erifila's forgiveness and restored to her all he has robbed her of. In order to make some sense of this, Lope has Fedra admit that she only pretended to be insane and in love with Floriano because Valerio had not responded to her love for him.

Now everything has been put to rights. All the people have found each other in accordance with their rank and station. Marriage sanctifies all relationships. Love, which is not understood in the normal world, can thrive only among the mad. Clearly, this comedia allows today a variety of ingenious interpretations, though surely it was conceived by Lope as nothing but a light and whimsical entertainment.

As Vossler said:

> The jest in this is that fully normal pairs of loving young people find themselves in circumstances and predicaments in which good sense and madness are so very close together that through misunderstandings, plays on words, and the most charming confusion, a variety of mischances ensues. This game is permeated by a lively sympathy of the irrationality of being in love, experiencing jealousy, but it is always kept in the background from which it can easily be lifted, and the laments of the truly sick are not taken too seriously. The director of the asylum, the doctor, the staff, and the inmates are all just figures in a farce.

The Madmen of Valencia is not a typical comedia. The situations and the atmosphere in it are new and unusual. It is true it has a lady and a cavalier as the principals, but other characters are original. The faithless Leonato is not a typical gracioso, although the lady's maid Laida might be reckoned in that category.

This well-known play has been performed frequently in the German-speaking world. Axel von Ambesser's staging at the Residenztheater in Munich in the 1957–1958 season was a huge success. The theater critic in the *Zeitung* praised Ambesser as the initiator of the cult of Lope. He said: "He strengthens the belief that the theater can also be a pleasure to its audience, a view that may sound a bit suspicious to those serious people who consider the theater only the temporal arm of philosophy." That critic also praised Ambesser's ability to steer between the pitfalls of a historical production and one in the style of the modern cabaret.

Another critic, however, felt that the effort to turn comedia, with its abundance of dialectic debate and its intentional alienation, into a modern, captivating play made for an unsuccessful production. Ambesser, who had readapted an adaptation, had produced not so much a finished play as a parade of clever witticisms and "not always Spanish" vaudeville gags. Every kind of humor was offered in this version, from surrealist to hullabaloo, and in between there was ample opportunity for melancholy moments.

It remains open to debate how far revisions that do not implement the dramatist's intentions can be justified to be relevant to the spirit of the times. In the case of a dramatist like Lope de Vega, who wrote dramas to be played, not literature to be read, few revisions, so long as they can be justified dramatically, would have been unacceptable to him.

In 1967, in the Frankfurt Theater am Turm, *The Madmen of Valencia* was offered as a work of social criticism, by Claus Peymann. Using a prose translation and a setting that departed from the baroque style, Peymann tried to catch the spirit of the work in a production of Brechtian preciseness. He succeeded far better with his love scenes that were almost monologues than in working out his self-imposed intention. From traditional productions one easily concludes that the whole world is a madhouse. But that the madhouse is also a snake pit, a horrible chamber of tortures, was first emphasized by Peymann in "the conclusive twitching and aggressive screaming of the inmates shut up in it." The normal ones have succumbed to real madness. Whoever wishes to rescue himself from the bonds of conformity must pretend to be mad. It is problematic, however, whether our contemporary need for such an interpretation gives us the right to alter Lope de Vega's approach so drastically.

Juan Ruiz de Alarcón y Mendoza (1580–1639)

Juan Ruiz de Alarcón y Mendoza, a humpback born in Mexico, was distrustful and irritable because of his deformity. He professed to despise the tastes of the rabble, but his comedias follow along the path blazed by Lope de Vega. Translated into many languages, his plays are the most typical examples of the popular cloak-and-sword comedias. If difference there be between his work and that of his fellow comedia writers it stems from Juan Ruiz's professed intention to offer his heroes as moral examples. I shall leave open the question whether this intent was, or indeed, could be realized in view of the agility and excitement of the plots he spun. Since, however, his primary interest was the dramatic presentation of a moral dilemma rather than the efficient staging of a situation, his plots are more concentrated, less many-faceted, than those of his contemporaries. He lacked the ability to write plays on demand, a shortcoming that the many who envied him, among whom can be counted some notable dramatists, scoffed at.

Tirso de Molina (ca. 1571–1648)

1571:   Gabriel Téllez is born in Madrid. He writes under the pen name Tirso de Molina. (It is also claimed that he was born in 1572, 1583, and 1584.) His parents are not known to us. The pen name he adopted may indicate his admiration for the great theologian Luis de Molina.

1600:   He enters the monastery of the Order of Mercy at Guadalajara.

1616–18: Lives and teaches in Haiti.

1626:   After this date he writes few comedias.

1646:   He begins writing a history of the monastery at Soria, in Old Castile.

1648:   On 12 March he dies at the Soria Monastery. At his death he is provincial of the order and superior of the house.

The most important of the later comedia writers (outside of Calderón) was the monk Gabriel Téllez, who wrote under the pen name of Tirso de Molina. He wrote three to four hundred plays, of which eighty-six are extant. His plays were among the most widely successful of the period. It does not contradict this observation to mention that not only were they frequently banned by the Inquisition but also were vehemently attacked by the learned. Although he was a member of the Order of Mercy for most of his life and was said to have faithfully performed its mission for many years in the new world, his plays exhibit a broadmindedness and a liberalness beyond that displayed by his contemporaries.

This liberalness probably resulted from the fact that he was not venturesome in his own life. He was an observer. He stood above the conflict and had a forgiving smile for everything. Among the writers of his day he had the keenest perception of human motives. He had more feeling for the uniqueness of the individual than for mankind as a whole. He acquired knowledge of people from the confessional. "He saw life in the world through the window of the cloister." To him the life of a man was both a subject for religious consideration and a demonstration of lovely gracefulness and charm.

The protagonists of his plays are generally women, whom he idealized. It is they who court their men and, literally, chased them. Vossler spoke of Tirso's uncanny insight into the heart of a woman. His plays were aimed at the bigotry that is prevalent. It is precisely this combination of a spiritual vocation, taken seriously, and of a relatively easygoing morality projected in art that is characteristic of a period when religion and morals did not yet coincide, as they were to do in the nineteenth century.

Tirso wrote parts for himself in many of his plays.

Unlike writers of character dramas in later centuries, he did not cast himself as a struggling or suffering hero. The role he wrote for himself was a sort of reflecting observer, perhaps a good-natured rustic wag, a shepherd, a swineherd, a sacristan, a secretary. He succeeded better than Lope de Vega in contriving complications out of which the much-desired happy ending could only be accomplished with the utmost dexterity. He shunned conventional plots.

Tirso's typical characters, essentially ironic, less lighthearted than those of Lope's, seem more modern to us. His popularity with theatergoers of the day was possibly due to the liking of every audience for excursions into the afterlife, especially with exciting complications, and to his predilection for the eerie.

A subject such as the Don Juan saga, which requires knowledge of human nature as well as the mastery of theatrical situations in order to present it with dramatic impact, practically forced itself on him. In his great play, *The Trickster of Seville and the Stone Guest*, Don Juan gets no quarter. He is characterized as a monster of selfishness and ruthlessness. That a life is being destroyed so that he may satisfy a passing surge of lust is a matter of no consequence to him. No deception or stratagem that will get his victim into his bed is below him. The plight of the women, who fall into his clutches with love and trust, is offered so sympathetically by Tirso that the spectator feels relief when the stone hand of the comendador crushes out an existence dedicated to devastating any human being, male and female, that lies in his path.

Tirso himself is said to have put little value on his writing skill and still less on his glory. He wrote only for his own satisfaction and possibly also to supplement his earnings. When we consider that for whole decades he wrote nothing at all because he was beset with hostility and persecution, his three hundred to four hundred plays are relatively no less a phenomenon than the fifteen hundred attributed to Lope de Vega.

Some of the charm and flavor of the comedias can be gleaned from the following description of one of Tirso de Molina's greatest comedias: *Don Gil Green Hose*.

Don Gil Green Hose

The drama of entanglement that Lope de Vega mastered so incomparably was raised by Tirso de Molina to the level of the burlesque and the improbable. It was accepted on the stage by the Spanish audience as if it reflected reality.

All the elements in Lope's technique of composing comedias, all the motifs he used—love, jealousy, honor, insult, duels, serenades under balconies, especially the disguises and the confusion of identity, which are among the most frequently exercised of the devices of their kind—are artfully intertwined in Tirso's master comedy, which is still being frequently performed in Europe. It amuses and amazes its audience. If any single play of the golden age exhibits all the carefree pointlessness of Spanish comedia, then it is Tirso's *Don Gil Green Hose*. We must accept it for what it is—a mad, naive, unrestrained but well crafted, nimble, and clever work of theater.

The comedias of Tirso de Molina demonstrate that the theater is capable of outmaneuvering our reasonable judgments, without the necessity of transporting us into the realm of metaphysics or surrealism. He makes the unlikely seem likely on the stage. He makes the world of illusion acceptable and welcome through the turbulence of surprise effects, one of which follows hot on the heel of the other. The "alteration of the situation" that is one of the basic elements of Spanish comedia reaches new heights in Tirso's work.

This play, *Don Gil Green Hose*, was published in 1635 in the collected comedias of Tirso de Molina (volume four). It was probably written a few years earlier. Though set apart by its brilliance, the fact that this comedia has parallels with Tirso's *Opportunity Makes Thieves* indicates that it was formula writing of a certain kind. We do know that Tirso de Molina regarded his playwriting as only a sideline. A resume of the plot would be extremely difficult and basically to no purpose for no enumeration of the external events would even approach doing justice to the charm that captures the audience's heart completely. The satisfactory outcome is assumed but the audience is maintained in a state of tension until the final solution is revealed.

As so often in Tirso's plays, by contrast to those of most of the other Spanish dramatists, women are given active parts. Doña Juana permitted Don Martín to possess her after he promised to marry her. Now, after he has proved unfaithful to her, she endeavors to win back his love. (It is interesting to note that in Lope de Vega's comedias the ladies of high rank are almost always virgins.)

Juana follows Martín secretly to Madrid, where, as his father wishes, he plans to marry the rich Inés. He has assumed the name of Don Gil. Juana disguises herself in men's attire, calls herself Don Gil (of the green hose, on account of her costume). She succeeds in making Inés fall in love with her. In between, however, she wears feminine garments and calls herself

Elvira. She manages to accuse her lover Martín of treachery with Inés, but conveys to him through a messenger the news of her death (Juana, that is) in a convent in childbirth. The high point of this mix-up is her idea of letting it be known that Elvira is Don Gil's beloved.

In the most famous scene in the play, four Don Gils in green hose come in under Inés's balcony: her scorned lover, Don Juan; the faithless Don Martín; Juana; and a disguised female friend of Inés, who has also fallen in love with the false Don Gil. Juana's father now appears. Everything is cleared up. The guilty Don Martín is forgiven. Three happy couples are united in marriage: Juana and her Martín; Inés and her Don Juan, and Inés's friend and a Don Antonio, who for the sake of the happy ending is introduced just in time as the hitherto rejected suitor of this maiden.

The gracioso of the play reflects: "Only a woman could create so fearful a mix-up." Here the gracioso is a reasoning observer. He delivers comments from his hiding place, as, for example, when he calls out, like a blusterer, to the four Don Gils who appear, "death to all Don Gils," but without taking part in the ensuing brawl himself.

The characters, in spite of their originality, conform to the cast in the typical cloak-and-sword comedias: four ladies and four cavaliers, a true gracioso, an old faithful retainer, the father, and the necessary auxiliary roles, such as the bailiff and a lawyer.

The scene of the action is again under the balcony of the house of the adored one or on Madrid's fashionable promenade where the loving couples meet. Inserts of dance and probably song, woven organically into the script, enhance the theatrical effect. Naive dramatic devices, such as the accidental loss of letters that fall by chance into the hands of the rival woman, are accepted without reflection. Even such scenes as overheard conversations, the most elementary stuff of comedy, are not lacking.

The first performance was in 1617. *Don Gil Green Hose* is the best-loved Spanish comedia in contemporary Germany. The production of this work presents great difficulties for the director and producer, but no matter what the interpretation, the play almost invariably wins warm audience approval. To give just one example, in Heidelberg in the 1951–1952 season, it was staged as an example of old Spanish life and world outlook by Heinz Dietrich, who refrained from making it a satire on a farce.

In summer 1964 the Royal Shakespeare Theatre produced this comedia under the title *Don Gil in the Green Stockings*. This production, directed by Clifford Williams, is said to have been the first British production of a Tirso de Molina play.

Antonio Coello y Ochos (1611–1652)

The cloak-and-sword play became a routinized type of comedia with Antonio Coello. Coello wrote a great deal in collaboration with others, among whom were such major dramatists as Calderón, Francisco de Rojas-Zorrilla, Luis Vélez de Guevara, Juan Pérez de Montalbán, and Antonio de Solís y Rivadeneyra. Such collaboration became necessary as the demand for new plays increased.

Coello also wrote topical plays, such as *Your Life for Your Queen*, which is based on the story of the relationship between Elizabeth and Essex. It has been ascribed by some to Philip V. He also wrote comedias in which the complications seem to be unduly contrived.

As Joseph Gregor pointed out, Coello's characters are not the type in the early cloak-and-sword comedias that so charmed the audience. It was these characters that raised them above the level of the rising Italian *commedia dell'arte* style. His characters are seen more as individual personalities, more individualized:

> In the old sequence: lover, friend, maiden, amorous old lady, crafty servant, old blusterer. They are constantly rearranged in new groupings in their entanglements in the newer comedy. It had long ago been made clear how the knightly youth, the jealous beauty, the noble, piqued old man, would conduct themselves, so the only suspense for the audience lay in the tortuous interplay of their motives, not in the sentiments themselves.

Agustín Moreto y Cabaña
(1618–1668)

1618:   Born in Madrid, the son of Agustín Moreto and Violante Cabaña. His parents were probably of Italian extraction.

1634–37:   Studies in Alcalá.

1639:   Receives his first diploma.

1642:   Receives his preliminary consecration and a church position in Mondéjar.

1649:   By now he has written the greater portion of his plays. He becomes a member of the Castilian Academy and one of the circle

around Calderón, the Calderón school. He
is soon regarded as one of the best of them.

1654: Twelve of his plays are published in the
first collected volume of his comedias.

1656: He moves to Seville.

1657: Is consecrated as a priest and becomes
manager of the almshouse in Madrid.

1668: Dies 28 October. Buried in a potter's field.

Don Agustín Moreto y Cabaña, the last important
representative of the Spanish drama in the golden age,
was both an excellent playwright and producer. His
technical proficiency made up for his limited creative
gift. Emerging from the circle around Calderón, the
so-called Calderón school, he was its outstanding
member. In contrast with his predecessors, his moralistic and didactic purpose outweighs any interest in
providing for mere entertainment. Only Alarcón
before him had made an effort in this direction, but
that approach met with only limited success. He
wrote thirty-two comedias.

Moreto, indeed an offspring of the new era, was
partly influenced by the new French teachings of the
supremacy of pure reason. Even his cloak-and-sword
plays show us distinctly the transition from the situation comedy to the comedy of character. The old
values, especially the concept of honor, no longer play
the decisive role. The determining issue is the personal
character of the hero.

It is worthy of note that a distinguished nineteenth-
century interpreter of theatrical movements, the
French critic Alfred Gassier, named Moreto's comedia
Answer Scorn with Scorn the most perfect example of
all comedias. In this play a Spanish dramatist began to

move in the direction of French taste, which was to become the fashion for future centuries.

The setting of Moreto's plays in one location is characteristic, an approach to observing the three Aristotelian unities.

Answer Scorn with Scorn

Although Moreto was only eighteen years younger than Calderón, his work obviously belongs to a newer era. Out of his fifteen comedias *Answer Scorn with Scorn* is just about the only one to survive in the European theater. This play first appeared in print in 1654, soon after the time when it seemed to have been famous. Although it is based on Lope de Vega's *Women's Revenge* and three other works by him, it must be regarded as an original work because of its inner content and outward structure. Its influence on non-Spanish writers was great. Molière imitated this play in his comedy *The Princess of Elis*. Carlo Gozzi drew from it for his comedy *The Philosopher Princess*. Raffaele Tauro utilized it for his *The Countess of Barcelona*.

A French critic in the late nineteenth century called it the most perfect comedia of all. It is just this praise given in the late nineteenth century that proves the distance from the earlier Spanish comedia, which has not been afforded such distinction. Moreto's play reflects the taste of the later period much more accurately. We do not find in it the qualities that are so strange in Lope's and Calderón's comedias, the prevalence of chance or miracle, the conscious confusion in the buildup, and the often illogical turns in the denouement. Here the character of the hero is more controlling than the occurrence of coincidence, there is more reason than marvel, and the buildup is clearly articulated. The influence of the more enlightened French spirit is perceptible. Man from being the object of the game is becoming the subject. He is not acted upon. He takes action himself.

The problem of free will, so much discussed in seventeenth-century Spain, "finds here a credible worldly answer, not a mere theological polemic" (Martin Franzbach). Or, from the woman's point of view, her unconscious wins out over her conscious intention. On first acquaintance with this play its outwardly old Spanish forms tend to obscure this difference, which is quite significant also from a theatrical point of view.

The action takes place in a park in Barcelona. The characters are ladies and cavaliers of the highest rank and their servants. The latter, male and female, both are typical graciosos. In fact a gracioso is virtually the leading character. More than in the plays of any other Spanish dramatist the gracioso holds all the threads in his hand. This is characteristic of all terminal times of eras of great theater. The merry figure, the favorite of the audience, pushes himself more and more into the center of the stage. He holds the interest of the onlooker most strongly for the longest time.

From the very start the motif of the play is seen to be different from the familiar Lope de Vega pattern. In a varied form one finds it twice in Shakespeare—in his *Much Ado about Nothing* and *The Taming of the Shrew*. Here, too, Doña Diana must be tamed, or, better said, her excessive pride broken, by the clever stratagem of her suitor. The unyielding must be converted into the devotedly loving one.

The Count of Barcelona has invited three young princes to attend the tournament at his court as he hopes to obtain a spouse for his daughter and to assure the land an heir. But Diana only cares for philosophy and wishes to have nothing to do with men. She prefers to be no man's subject. Polilla, the servant of Count Carlos, one of the suitors, persuades his master to repay like with like. However much he may be in love with Diana, he must act cold and indifferent. Carlos follows this advice. Polilla, disguised as a doctor, wins Diana's confidence, so that he can constantly keep his master informed of the situation and the views of the coy beauty.

Diana is annoyed by Carlos's indifference. It becomes a point of pride with her to evoke his love in order to humiliate him all the more when he does love her. Polilla promptly reports this intention to his master. By exercising the greatest willpower, Carlos resists the first affectionate approaches Diana makes to him. At a garden party where he is her escort, he abruptly avows his love for her. But he immediately comes to his senses and says that he made this declaration only as a test of her attitude. Her effort to attract him by her lute playing also fails. Carlos takes no notice of either the performance or the performer.

To spur her awakening affection, which Carlos learns of through Polilla, he informs her falsely that he has decided in favor of the lovely Cintia, one of her cousins. The despairing Diana knows no other way to get at him except through jealousy. She tells him untruthfully that she has decided to accept one of the other suitors as her husband. But this suitor and Cintia, who are in love with each other, play along with Polilla's plan.

Diana's father announces the betrothal of Carlos to

Cintia, and of Diana to the other suitor. This is too much for Diana. She feels she will surely die. This allows Carlos to drop his mask. Now everything proceeds to a happy ending. Diana's pride is conquered by the pangs of love. Polilla, without whose cunning the whole scheme would not have succeeded, marries the lady's maid Laura, to whom, in the mirror action reflecting the ruses of his master, he has been pretending all along to be indifferent.

This brief resume shows how much more straightforwardly Moreto's plot moves than do those in the dramas of his predecessors. The plot has no fanciful turns, no interlaced entanglements, other than those that occur through the natural actions of the characters. The lady's pride is opposed by her lover's acted pride. The one who pulls the strings is the gracioso who devised the practical stratagem that succeeded. The supporting roles, with the exception of that of the kindly disposed father, which is dramatically essential, are parallel to the principal roles.

The love pains of the protagonists are heightened by being set against the smoother love relationships of the other couple. The gracioso couple parallels the principal couple. It is only these four principal parts—the graciosos and Carlos and Diana—that are drawn in detail. The supporting roles are presented only in schematic outline. It is something of a paradox that the "objective" figures of the older comedias are more individually drawn than the "subjective" figures of the newer comedias. The play hardly differs from its predecessors in its outward format or in its quality. Both have lyrical interludes, musical intermezzos, and vocally sung presentation, all incorporated into the action. But in *Answer Scorn with Scorn* even the structure of the scenes is stricter and more consistent.

The folklore element that often seems improvisational in the older cloak-and-sword plays takes here a more elegant form where fantasy yields to reason.

It is significant that by the early 1800s *Answer Scorn with Scorn* had become a fixed item in the German repertory. A literary historian so typical of the nineteenth century as Johannes Scherr called it "psychologically the truest, most absorbing, most refined, most graceful comedia in Spanish literature." Even today it is among the most frequently produced of the comedias, in spite of the fact that it is the furthest removed from the spirit, and thereby from the amazing modernity, of the Spanish comedia. This may be due to the law of inertia, to which public taste is also subject. New styles are accepted only slowly. The psychological aspect and the refined clowning of this comedia seem to contemporary audiences to offer more than the more robust humor and the illogical quality of the older comedias.

Although most reviewers ascribe the popularity of this comedia to the talent of the directors who have handled it, we must recognize that the credit for this success goes to Moreto. In addition it is more to the theatergoer's taste than other cloak-and-sword comedias because of its straightforward plot and controlled dramatic action.

Many newspapers reported that "the most refined and gracious" production of Hans Thimig, in the Burgtheater in Vienna in 1946, was received with unrestrained applause of the audience. Thimig, with the utmost precision, created a production in the style of a graceful caricature, free of historic chitchat and literary experiment. It was said that the comedia had been transformed into a fairy tale. The actors' handling of word and movement, which was rigorously choreo-graphical but never constrictive, gave the theatergoer the impression he was watching porcelain marionettes in action.

This play was frequently presented outdoors. It is not without interest that little, intimate theaters also tried to produce it, though with little success.

All the productions reaffirm the prime importance of the gracioso in this play. Staging this play, which seems a simple enough matter, poses major problems to directors and actors. This was recognized over a century ago by Joseph Schreyvogel, who wrote: "The way these three principals are confronted with each other must, if they are well played, make an effective impression on the stage, but it cannot be denied that a perfect performance of this dramatic concert piece is one of the most difficult tasks in the whole art of acting."

BIBLIOGRAPHY

1. WORKS BY THE SPANISH DRAMATISTS

The Algerian Captives—Los cautivos ó Los esclavos de Argél (Vega).

Answer Scorn with Scorn—El desdén con el desdén (Moreto). Translation, "Love's Victory, or The School for Pride," by G. Hyde, London and Edinburgh: Hurst, 1825.

Aquilana (Torres Naharro).

Belisa's Pruderies—Melindres de Belisa (Vega).

The Book of Good Love—Libro de buen amor (Ruiz de Hita). Translation by Elisha K. Kane, Chapel Hill: University of North Carolina Press, 1968.

The Buttercup—La francesilla (Vega).

La Celestina (Rojas). Translation, "The Spanish Bawd," by James Mabbe, London, 1631. Revised by Eric Bentley, ed., in *The Classic Theatre III*, New York: Doubleday, 1959. See also translation by Mack H. Singleton, Madison: University of Wisconsin Press, 1958.

The Customs of Algeria—El trato de Argél (Cervantes). Verse translation, "The Commerce of Algiers," by W. J. Gyll, London: Murray, 1870.

The Dog in the Manger—El perro del hortelano (Vega). Translation by Jill Booty, in *Five Plays*, New York: Hill & Wang, 1961.

The Divorce Judge—El juez de los divorcios (Cervantes). Translation, "The Judge of the Divorce Court," in *The Genius of the Spanish Theater*, edited by Robert O'Brien, New York: New American Library, 1964.

Don Gil Green Hose—Don Gil de las· calzas verdes (Tirso de Molina).

La Dorotea (Vega).

The Enamored Minx—La discreta enamorada (Vega).

Fuente Ovejuna (Vega). Translation by Jill Booty, in *Five Plays*, New York: Hill & Wang, 1961. See also verse translation, "The Sheep Well," by Roy Campbell, in *The Classic Theatre III*, edited by Eric Bentley, New York: Doubleday, 1959.

The Galician Beauty—La lindona de Galicit (Montalbán).

The Gardener's Dog, see *The Dog in the Manger*.

The Golden Fleece—El vellocino de oro (Vega).

Hymen—Comedia himenea (Torres Naharro). Translation by W. Chambers, in *The Drama: Its History, Literature and Influence in Civilization*, edited by A. Bates, vol. 6, London: 1903–1904.

Inés Pereira (Vicente).

Jacinta (Torres Naharro).

The Jewess of Toledo—Las paces de los reyes y judía de Toledo (Vega).

Loving Not Knowing Whom—Amar sin saber a quién (Vega).

The Madmen of Valencia—Los locos de Valencia (Vega).

The New Art of Writing Plays—Arte nuevo de hacer comedias en este tiempo (Vega). Translation by W. T. Brewster, New York: Columbia University Dramatic Museum, 1914.

Not So Stupid After All—La dama boba (Vega). Translation, "The Idiot Lady," by William I. Oliver, in *The Genius of the Spanish Theater*, edited by

Robert O'Brien, New York: New American Library, 1964.

Opportunity Makes Thieves—La villano de vallescas (Tirso de Molina).

The Palace Disordered—El palacio confuso (Vega).

The Peasant in His Nook—El villano en su rincón (Vega).

Pilgrim in His Own Land—Peregrino en su patria (Vega).

Pretense Becomes Truth—Lo fingido veradero (Vega).

The Prince of Illescas—El infantón de Illescas (Vega).

The Salamanca Cave—La cueva de Salamanca (Cervantes). Translation, "The Cave of Salamanca," by Willis K. Jones, in *Spanish One-Act Plays in English*, Dallas, Texas: Tardy Publishing Co., 1934.

Serafina (Torres Naharro).

The Sheep Well, see *Fuente Ovejuna*.

The Shoemaker and the King—El zapatero y el Rey (Vega).

The Siege of Numantia—La Numancia (Cervantes). Verse translation, "Numantia: A Tragedy," by Roy Campbell, in *The Classic Theatre III*, edited by Eric Bentley, New York: Doubleday, 1959.

Sir Miracle Comes a Cropper—El caballero del milagro (Vega).

Soldatesca (Torres Naharro).

The Temptation of Helen—La prueba de Elena (Vega).

The Theater of Wonders—El retablo de las maravillas (Cervantes).

Those Who Were Deceived—De los enganados (Rueda).

The Trickster of Seville—El burlador de Sevilla (Tirso de Molina). Verse translation, "The Love-Rogue," by Harry Kemp, New York: Lieber and Lewis, 1923. See also verse translation, "The Trickster of Seville and the Guest of Stone," by Roy Campbell, in

The Classic Theatre III, edited by Eric Bentley, New York: Doubleday, 1959. And "The Playboy of Seville," by Walter Starkie, in *Eight Spanish Plays of the Golden Age*, New York: Modern Library, 1964.

The Ugly Beauty—La hermosa fea (Vega).

The Waters of Madrid—El acero de Madrid (Vega).

Women's Revenge—La vengadora de las mujeres (Vega).

Your Life for Your Queen—Dar la vida por su dama (Coello).

2. COLLECTED EDITIONS OF THE WORKS

Juan del Encina. *Teatro completo*. Edited by M. Cañete. 1893.

———. *Canciones*. Edited by A. J. Battastessa. Buenos Aires, 1941.

Gil Vicente. *Copilaçam de todas obras de Gil Vicente*. Edited by L. and P. Vicente. 1562.

———. *Obras*. Edited by J. Mendes dos Remédios. 3 vols. Coimbra, 1907–1914.

———. *Four Plays*. Translated by A. F. G. Bell. Cambridge, England, 1920.

———. *The Ship of Hell*. Translated by A. F. Gerald. Watford, England, 1929.

———. *Obras completas*. Edited by T. Braga. 6 vols. Lisbon, 1942–44.

Bartolomé de Torres Naharro. *Propalladia*. Naples, 1517.

———. *Propalladia*. Edited by M. Cañete and M. Menéndez y Pelayo. 2 vols. Madrid, 1880–1900.

———. *Propalladia and Other Works*. Edited by J. E. Gillet. 3 vols. Bryn Mawr, Penn., 1942–51.

Lope de Rueda. *Obras*. Edited by the Marquis of Fuensanta del Valle. 2 vols. Madrid, 1895–96.
———. *Obras*. Edited by E. Cotarelo y Mori. 2 vols. Madrid, 1908.

Miguel de Cervantes. *Complete Works*. Edited by James Fitzmaurice-Kelly. 1901–1903.
———. *Obras completas*. Edited by A. Bonilla y San Martín and R. Schevill. 14 vols. 1914–15.
———. *Obras completas*. Edited by Angel Valbuena Prat. 1943.
———. *The Interludes of Cervantes*. Edited and translated by S. Griswold Morley. 1948.
———. *Interludes*. Translated by Edwin Honig. New York, 1964.

Lope de Vega. *Comedias*. 25 vols. 1604–1647.
———. *Colección de las obras sueltas*. 21 vols. 1776–79.
———. *Obras de Lope de Vega*. Edited by M. Menéndez y Pelayo. 15 vols. Madrid, 1890–1913.
———. *Four Plays*. Edited and translated by J. G. Underhill. New York, 1936.
———. *Teatro escogido de Lope de Vega*. Edited by F. C. Sáinz de Robles. Madrid, 1958.
———. *Five Plays*. Edited by R. D. F. Pring-Mill. Translated by Jill Booty. New York, 1961.

Juan Ruiz de Alarcón. *Parte primera*. Madrid, 1628. *Parte segunda*. Barcelona, 1634.
———. *Comedias*. Edited by J. E. Hartzenbusch. Biblioteca de autores españoles 20. Madrid, 1931.
———. *Obras completas*. Edited by A. Millares Carlo. 2 vols. Mexico City, 1958.

Tirso de Molina. *Comedias escogidas*. Edited by J. E. Hartzenbusch. Biblioteca de autores españoles 5. Madrid, 1850.

Tirso de Molina. *Obras dramáticas completas*. Edited by B. de los Ríos. 2 vols. Madrid, 1946–58.

Agustín Moreto y Cabaña. *Comedias*. 3 vols. 1654, 1676, 1681.
————. *Obras escogidas*. Edited by L. Fernández Guerra y Orbe. Biblioteca de autores españoles 39. Madrid, 1856.

3. WORKS ABOUT THE SPANISH COMEDIA WRITERS

Gil Vicente

A. Broamcamp Freire. *Vida e obras de Gil Vicente*. Oporto, 1921.
L. Keates. *The Court Theatre of Gil Vicente*. Lisbon, 1962.

Miguel de Cervantes

Sebastian Juan Arbo. *Cervantes: The Man and His Time*. Translated by Ilsa Barea. New York: Vanguard Press, 1955.
Américo Castro. *El pensamiento de Cervantes*. 2nd, revised ed. Barcelona: Noguer, 1972.
Alban K. Forcione. *Cervantes' Christian Romance*. New Jersey: Princeton University Press, 1972.
Francisco Navarro Ledesma. *Cervantes: The Man and the Genius*. Translated and revised by Don and Gabriella Bliss. New York: Charterhouse Books, 1972.

Lope de Vega

Hugo Albert Rennert. *The Life of Lope de Vega*. Philadelphia: Campion & Co., 1904.

Rudolph Schevill. *The Dramatic Art of Lope de Vega.* Berkeley: University of California Press, 1918.

S. G. Morley, and C. Bruerton. *The Chronology of Lope de Vega's "Comedias."* New York, 1940.

A. Zamora Vicente. *Lope de Vega.* 1961.

Angel Valbuena Prat. "A Freudian Character in Lope de Vega." *Drama Review* 7, no. 1 (1962–63):44–54.

J. A. Parker, and A. M. Fox, eds. *Lope de Vega Studies (1937–1962): A Critical Survey and Annotated Bibliography.* Toronto: University of Toronto Press, 1964.

F. C. Hayes. *Lope de Vega.* New York, 1967.

Tirso de Molina

R. Menéndez Pidal. *Estudios literarios.* 1938.

I. L. McClelland. *Tirso de Molina: Studies in Dramatic Realism.* Liverpool, 1948.

A. H. Bushee. *Three Centuries of Tirso de Molina.* Philadelphia, 1954.

Agustín Moreto y Cabaña

Ruth Lee Kennedy. *The Dramatic Art of Moreto.* Smith College Studies in Modern Languages 13. Northampton, Mass., 1932.

F. P. Casa. *The Dramatic Craftsmanship of Moreto.* Cambridge, Mass., 1966.

General Studies

Hugo Albert Rennert. *The Spanish Stage in the Time of Lope de Vega.* New York: Hispanic Society, 1909.

James Fitzmaurice-Kelly. *A New History of Spanish Literature.* New York: Oxford University Press, 1926.

Somerset Maugham. *Don Fernando.* Garden City, N. Y.: Doubleday, 1935.

Stephen Gilman. *The Art of "La Celestina."* Madison: University of Wisconsin Press, 1956.

María Rosa Lida de Malkiel. *Two Spanish Masterpieces: The Book of Good Love and The Celestina.* Urbana: University of Illinois Press, 1962.

Stephen Gilman. *The Spain of Fernando de Rojas: The Intellectual and Social Landscape of "La Celestina."* Princeton, N. J.: Princeton University Press, 1972.

INDEX